# iNTERCOM 2000

**Anna Uhl Chamot**

**Joan Baker de Gonzalez**

**Isobel Rainey de Diaz**

**Richard Yorkey**

Heinle & Heinle Publishers
A Division of Wadsworth, Inc.
Boston, Massachusetts 02116

**Publisher:** Stanley J. Galek
**Editorial Director:** Christopher Foley
**Project Editor:** Anita L. Raducanu
**Content Editor:** Margot Gramer
**Assistant Editor:** Erik Gundersen

**Production Supervisor:** Patricia Jalbert
**Production Manager:** Erek Smith
**Designed and Produced by:** Publishers' Graphics Inc.
**Illustrations for Units 1-6:** Linda Kelen
**Prepress Color and Integration:**
FinalCopy Electronic Publishing Services
**Cover:** The Graphics Studio/Gerry Rosentswieg

## Acknowledgments

The authors and publisher would like to acknowledge the contributions of the following individuals who reviewed the *Intercom 2000* program at various stages of development and who offered many helpful insights and suggestions:

- Mary J. Erickson and Galen Shaney, *English Language Institute, University of Texas, Pan American*
- Toni Sachs Hadi, *New York City Board of Education*
- Katy Cox, *Casa Thomas Jefferson, Brasília, Brazil*
- Ronald A. Reese, *Long Beach (CA) Unified School District*
- Lúcia de Aragão, Sonia Godoy, and Rosa Erlichman, *União Cultural, São Paulo, Brazil*
- Peggy Kazkaz, *William Rainey Harper College*
- Roland G. Axelson, Diane Hazel, and Mary Wayne Pierce, *Hartford (CT) Public Schools*
- Keith A. Buchanan, *Fairfax County (VA) Public Schools*

# Contents

| COMMUNICATION | GRAMMAR | SKILLS |
|---|---|---|

| COMMUNICATION | GRAMMAR | SKILLS |
|---|---|---|

| COMMUNICATION | GRAMMAR | SKILLS |
|---|---|---|

| COMMUNICATION | GRAMMAR | SKILLS |
|---|---|---|

# Intercom 2000

# The People

Adela, Lisa, Tom, Bob, and Sam Logan

Elinor, Mike, Liz, Joyce, Ted, and Howard Young

Melanie, Pablo, Ana, and Carlos Nava, and Maria Gomez de Nava

Gino Leone

Gloria Rivera

Cristina Silva

Nhu Trinh

Toshio Ito

Sekila Manzikala

UNIT **1**

COMMUNICATION
Introducing yourself ▪ Identifying a person:
name, occupation ▪ Asking about name,
occupation ▪ Greetings and farewells

PRACTICAL LANGUAGE
Classroom instructions ▪
Numbers 1-20

GRAMMAR
Subject pronouns: *I, you, he, she, it* ▪
Demonstrative pronoun: *this* ▪
Be: *am, is, are* ▪ Indefinite articles

# Welcome to Winfield

*This is Winfield High School in Winfield, New York. The boys are Bob Logan and Mike Young. The girl is Gloria Rivera.*

| BOB: | Hi. Are you new here? |
|---|---|
| GLORIA: | Yes, I am. I'm from New York. |
| BOB: | Oh. Welcome to Winfield. I'm Bob Logan. |
| MIKE: | And I'm Mike Young. |
| GLORIA: | Nice to meet you, Bob. Nice to meet you, Mike. My name is Gloria Rivera. |
| BOB: | Nice to meet you, Gloria. |
| MIKE: | Yeah, nice to meet you, Gloria. |

# 1 Presentation 🔲

### Greetings and introductions

> I'm = I am

MIKE:   Hello.  I'm Mike Young.
GLORIA: Hi.  Nice to meet you, Mike.
        My name is Gloria Rivera.
MIKE:   Nice to meet you, Gloria.

# 2 Pronunciation 🔲

**Pronounce these sentences with falling intonation.**

**1.** Hi.  I'm Bob Logan.

**2.** My name is Gloria Rivera.

**3.** Nice to meet you.

# 3 Interaction

**Introduce yourself to your classmates.**

A: | Hi. | I'm _____ .
   | Hello. |
B: Nice to meet you, _____ .
   | I'm | _____ .
   | My name is |
A: Nice to meet you, _____ .

## 4 Presentation

### Identifying a person: name, occupation

> he's = he is
> she's = she is

A

This is Tom Logan.
He's a travel agent.

B

This is Adela Logan.
She's a homemaker.

C

This is Sam Logan.
He's a mechanic.

D

This is Lisa Logan.
She's a student.

E

This is Gino Leone.
He's a cook.

F

This is Cristina Silva.
She's a restaurant cashier.

## 5 Practice

**Point to and identify one of the characters in 4.**

| This is | _____ . |
| She's | a |
| He's | _____ . |

## 6 Vocabulary in Context 🔊

### Occupations

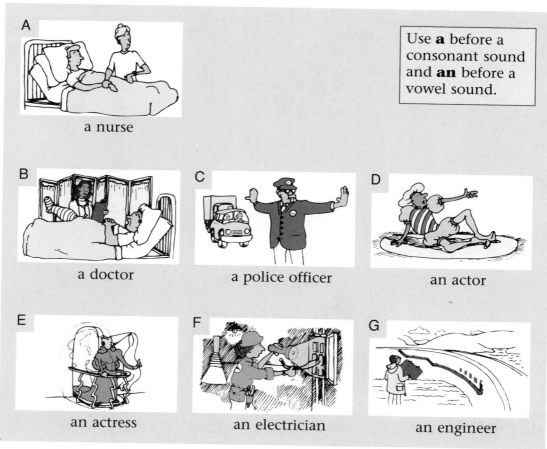

A

a nurse

> Use **a** before a consonant sound and **an** before a vowel sound.

B

a doctor

C

a police officer

D

an actor

E

an actress

F

an electrician

G

an engineer

## 7 Pronunciation 🔊

**Emphasize the syllable with the dot.**

• student    • cashier    • homemaker    mechanic •

• actor    police •    • officer    Cristina •

• actress    electrician •

• doctor

## 8 Presentation

### Asking about occupation

A: Is Tom a travel agent?
B: Yes, he is.
A: Is Adela a mechanic?
B: No, she isn't. She's a homemaker.

isn't = is not

## 9 Pronunciation

**Repeat these sentences.**

1. Is Lisa a student?

Yes, she is.

2. Is Gino a police officer?

No, he isn't. He's a cook.

## 10 Practice

**Ask and answer questions about the *Intercom 2000* characters on page 6.**

Adela / mechanic

A: Is Adela a mechanic?
B: No, she isn't. She's a homemaker.

1. Tom / actor
2. Lisa / nurse
3. Adela / homemaker
4. Sam / electrician
5. Gloria / engineer

6. Bob / student
7. Gino / police officer
8. Adela / actress
9. Cristina / doctor
10. Bob / engineer

## 11 Presentation

### Asking about name and occupation

who's = who is
it's = it is

A: Who's this?
B: It's Gino.
A: What does he do?
B: He's a cook.

## 12 Pronunciation

**Repeat these sentences.**

**1.** Who's this?

It's Lisa Logan.

**2.** What does she do?

She's a student.

## 13 Practice

Work with a partner. Point to an *Intercom 2000* character on page 6. Ask and answer questions. Follow the conversation model in *11*.

## 14 Presentation

### Asking for and giving personal information

what's = what is

JUDY: What's your name?
PABLO: My name is Pablo Vega.
JUDY: What do you do, Pablo?
PABLO: I'm an artist.

## 15 Interaction

**A. Talk to another person in your class.**

> A: What's your name?
> B: My name is _____ .
> A: What do you do _____ ?
> B: I'm | a | _____ .
>        | an |

**B. Introduce yourself or your partner to the class.**

> **You:**
>     My name is _____ .
>     I'm | a | _____ .
>        | an |
>
> **Your partner:**
>     This is _____ .
>     | She's | a | _____ .
>     | He's | an |

## 16 Presentation

### Greetings and farewells (formal)

|  | 4:00 AM-12:00 noon | 12:01 PM-6:00 PM | 6:01 PM-11:00 PM |
|---|---|---|---|
| **Greetings:** | Good morning, Mrs. Wilson. | Good afternoon, Ms. Barker. | Good evening, Mr. Mann. |
| **Farewells:** | Good-bye. | Good-bye. \| See you this evening. \| See you tonight. | Good night. \| See you tomorrow. |

A

BOB: Good morning, Mrs. Wilson. How are you today?
MRS. WILSON: Good morning, Bob. I'm fine, thank you.

B

BOB: Good-bye, Mrs. Wilson. See you tomorrow.
MRS. WILSON: Good-bye, Bob.

## 17 Interaction

Practice saying *hello* and *good-bye* to a person who is not a close friend. Change the time of day and use the titles *Mrs.*, *Ms.*, or *Mr.*

A: Good _____ , _____ .
How are you today?
B: Good _____ , _____ .
I'm fine, thank you.
A: Good-bye, _____ .
See you _____ .
B: Good-bye, _____ .

## 18 Presentation

### Greetings and farewells (informal)

A How's everything?

how's = how is

Great!    Fine.    OK.

B

BOB:  Hi, Mike.  How's everything?
MIKE: Fine, thanks.  How's everything with *you*?
BOB:  OK.

MIKE: Well... Bye, Bob.  See you later.
BOB:  Yeah, take care.

## 19 Interaction

**Practice saying *hello* and *good-bye* to a close friend or a person your age.**

A:  Hi,  _____ .  How's everything?
B:  _____ .  How's everything with *you*?
A:  _____ !
B:  Well... Bye,  _____ .  See you  _____ .
A:  _____ .  Take care.

## 20 Reentry

**Complete the sentences with *am*, *is*, or *are*.**

**1.** Hi. I _____ Gloria Rivera.

**2.** This _____ Sam Logan.
He _____ a mechanic.

**3.** Good morning, Mr. Mann.
How _____ you?

**4.** This _____ Adela Logan.
She _____ a homemaker.

# Practical Language

## 1 Presentation

### Classroom Instructions

1. Listen to me.
2. Say this word.
3. Take out a piece of paper.
4. Give me your paper.
5. Open your books.
6. Look at the pictures.
7. Close your books.
8. | Put away your books.
   | Put your books away. |

> **Negative instruction:**
> Don't open your books.
> Don't look at the pictures.

## 2 Presentation and Practice

### Numbers from 1 - 20

| | | | |
|---|---|---|---|
| 1 | one | 11 | eleven |
| 2 | two | 12 | twelve |
| 3 | three | 13 | thirteen |
| 4 | four | 14 | fourteen |
| 5 | five | 15 | fifteen |
| 6 | six | 16 | sixteen |
| 7 | seven | 17 | seventeen |
| 8 | eight | 18 | eighteen |
| 9 | nine | 19 | nineteen |
| 10 | ten | 20 | twenty |

> **Pronunciation:**
> **Emphasize the syllables**
> **with the dots.**
> ● ●
> fifteen
>   ●
> twenty

**Say a number. Your partner will say the next number.**

> A: eight
> B: nine

UNIT
**2**

COMMUNICATION
Introducing people to each other ▪
Identifying people and asking for their
names ▪ Talking about family
PRACTICAL LANGUAGE
Numbers 21-120 ▪ The alphabet

GRAMMAR
Subject Pronouns: *we, they* ▪
Demonstratives: *this, that, these* ▪
Possessive Adjectives ▪ Coordination: *and* ▪
Noun Plurals ▪ Noun Singular Possessive

# This Is My Family

*Mike and Gloria are at a Chinese restaurant in Winfield.*

MIKE:     Here's a picture of my family at the beach. These
are my parents. This is my brother, Ted. These are my
sisters, Liz and Joyce.

GLORIA:   What a nice family! And who are these people?

MIKE:     My friends, Gino Leone and Cristina Silva. He's a cook
at the Roma. She's a cashier there.
Oh. ... Look, Gloria. Here comes my brother.

TED:     Hi, Mike. How's everything?

MIKE:   Fine. How's everything with
you?

TED:     OK. *(to Gloria)* Hi.

MIKE:   Oh, excuse me. Ted, this is
Gloria Rivera. Gloria, this
is my brother, Ted.

GLORIA: Nice to meet you, Ted.

TED:     Nice to meet *you*, Gloria.

# 1 Presentation

## Introducing people to each other

| | |
|---|---|
| YUKO: | Hi, May. How's everything? |
| MAY: | OK. *(to Bill)* Hi. |
| YUKO: | Oh, excuse me, May. This is Bill Johnson. Bill, this is May Lin. |
| MAY: | Nice to meet you, Bill. |
| BILL: | Nice to meet *you*, May. |

# 2 Interaction

**Form a group of three. Practice introducing one student to another.**

| | |
|---|---|
| A: | *(to B)* Hi, _____ . How's everything? |
| B: | _____ . *(to C)* Hi. |
| A: | Oh, excuse me, _____ . This is _____ . _____ , this is _____ . |
| B: | Nice to meet you, _____ . |
| C: | Nice to meet *you*, _____ . |

**Presentation** 📼

### Identifying people with *that*

that's = that is

A:  Who's that?
B:  That's Howard Young.
    He's an engineer.

That's Elinor Young.
She's a doctor.

That's Liz Young.
She's a telephone operator.

That's Joyce Young.
She's a student.

That's Mike Young.
He's a student.

That's Ted Young.
He's a student.

## 4  Practice

Practice with a partner.  Ask about and name the people in *3*.  Follow the conversation model.

**Presentation** 🎙️

### Identifying people and asking for their names

**A. *Identifying your family***

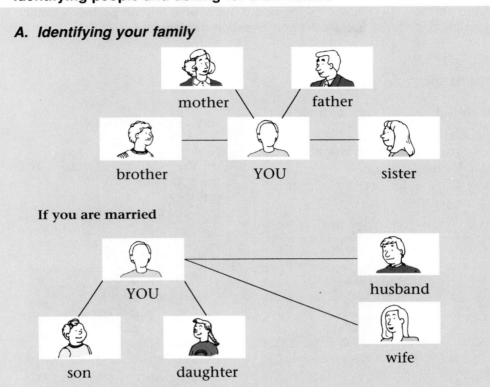

If you are married

**B. *Asking for people's names***

| GLORIA: | Who's this? |
| MIKE: | That's my sister. |
| GLORIA: | What's her name? |
| MIKE: | Joyce. |

| GLORIA: | And who's this? |
| MIKE: | That's my brother. |
| GLORIA: | What's his name? |
| MIKE: | Ted. |

## 6 Practice

Draw a diagram of your family or bring a picture of your family to class. Work with a partner. Take turns asking about the people in your partner's family diagram or picture. Follow the conversation models in *5*.

## 7 Presentation

### Asking about groups of people

| | |
|---|---|
| Use **these people** to ask about two or more people.<br>Use **they're** to identify two or more people.<br><br>they're = they are | **Noun plurals:**<br>brothers /z/   sisters   friends<br>**Irregular plurals:**<br>one person / two people<br>my child / my  children<br>                      kids (*informal*) |

**A**

GLORIA: Who are these people?
MIKE: They're my sisters.
GLORIA: What are their names?
MIKE: This is Liz.
This is Joyce.

**B**

GLORIA: Who are these people?
MIKE: They're my parents.
GLORIA: What are their names?
MIKE: Elinor and Howard Young.

**C**

GLORIA: Who are these people?
MIKE: They're my friends?
GLORIA: What are their names?
MIKE: This is Gino Leone.
This is Cristina Silva.

**D**

MARY: Who are these people?
LIZ: They're my brothers and sisters.
MARY: What are their names?
LIZ: This is Mike. This is Ted.
This is Joyce.

## 8 Interaction

Draw stick figures of your friends and family or bring pictures to class. Work with a partner. Take turns asking about the people in your partner's pictures.

A: Who's this?
B: That's my _____ .
A: What's _____ ?
B: _____ .

Useful words:
boyfriend
girlfriend

A: Who are these people ?
B: They're my _____ .
A: What are _____ ?
B: This is _____ , and this is _____ .

## 9 Presentation

Introducing yourselves and identifying your children and friends

we're = we are

We're the Youngs.
These are our children.
Their names are Liz,
Mike, Ted, and Joyce.

## 10 Practice

With a classmate, take the roles of the Youngs or the Logans. Introduce yourselves. Identify your children or friends. Follow the conversation model in *9*.

1. Youngs / sons / Mike and Ted
2. Youngs / daughters / Liz and Joyce
3. Logans / sons / Sam and Bob
4. Logans / children / Sam, Bob, and Lisa
5. Logans / friends / Gino and Cristina

## 11 Presentation 📼

### Talking about family relationships

A

This is Ted's sister, Joyce.

> **Singular Possessive:**
> Add **'s** to a name to show relationship.

B

This is Mike's brother, Ted.

C

These are Liz's parents, Howard and Elinor Young.

## 12 Pronunciation 📼

### Pronounce these words.

|  | **No extra syllable** | **Extra syllable** |
|---|---|---|
| **A. Plural** | brother**s** <br> sister**s** <br> son**s** <br> daughter**s** <br> parent**s** | two hous**es**  |
| **B. Possessive** | Bob**'s** brother <br> Adela**'s** daughter <br> Ted**'s** sister, Joyce <br> Elinor**'s** daughter, Liz <br> Tom**'s** wife <br> Lisa**'s** father <br> Mike**'s** mother | Liz**'s** brother, Mike <br><br> Joyce**'s** mother |

## 13 Practice

Work with a partner. Point to a picture in Unit 1 or 2. Take turns identifying the people.

> A: Who's this?
> B: | That's Liz's brother, Mike.
>    | That's Elinor's son, Mike.
>    | That's Bob's friend, Mike.

## 14 Listening

Number your paper from 1-10. Listen and write the number or numbers of the person or people.

1   2   3   4   5   6

> YOU HEAR:  Mike's father
> WRITE:          4

## 15 Reentry

> **Contractions with *be***
> I'm = I am          we're = we are
> he's = he is        you're = you are
> she's = she is      they're = they are
> it's = it is

Complete these sentences with the correct form: *I'm, he's, she's, it's, we're, they're.*

1. My name is Bob Logan. _____ a student.
2. We are the Logans. _____ Bob's parents.
3. This is Sam Logan. _____ a mechanic.
4. This is Cristina Silva. _____ Gino's girlfriend.
5. These are the Youngs. _____ Mike's parents.

6. Who's this? _____ Mike's sister, Joyce.
7. This is Gloria Rivera. _____ Bob's new friend.
8. These are the Logans. _____ Sam's parents.
9. Who's this? _____ Joyce's brother, Ted.
10. This is Gino Leone. _____ a cook.


## 16 Reentry

| Possessive adjectives | |
|---|---|
| (I) | my |
| (you) | your |
| (he) | his |
| (she) | her |
| (we) | our |
| (they) | their |

**Complete the sentences with the correct possessive adjective.**

1. Hi. I'm Bob Logan. This is _____ father.
   _____ name is Tom.

2. Hi. I'm Mike Young. This is _____ mother.
   _____ name is Elinor.

3. Hi. I'm Bob Logan. These are _____ parents.
   _____ names are Tom and Adela Logan.

4. Hi. What's _____ name?

5. Hi. I'm Mike Young. These are _____ sisters.
   _____ names are Liz and Joyce.

6. Hi. We're the Logans. These are _____ children.
   _____ names are Sam, Bob, and Lisa.

7. This is Gino Leone. _____ girlfriend is Cristina.

8. This is Cristina Silva. _____ boyfriend is Gino.

9. These are the Logans. _____ children are Sam, Bob, and Lisa.

10. Hi. We're the Youngs. These are _____ children.
    _____ names are Liz, Mike, Ted, and Joyce.

# Practical Language

## 1 Presentation

### Numbers 21-120

| | | | |
|---|---|---|---|
| 21 | twenty-one | 50 | fifty |
| 22 | twenty-two | 60 | sixty |
| 23 | twenty-three | 70 | seventy |
| 24 | twenty-four | 80 | eighty |
| 25 | twenty-five | 90 | ninety |
| 26 | twenty-six | 100 | one hundred / a hundred |
| 27 | twenty-seven | | |
| 28 | twenty-eight | 101 | one hundred one / a hundred one |
| 29 | twenty-nine | 110 | one hundred ten / a hundred ten |
| 30 | thirty | | |
| 40 | forty | 120 | one hundred twenty / a hundred twenty |

**Pronunciation:
Emphasize the syllable with the dot.**

• twenty    twenty-one •

• thirty    thirty-two •

## 2 Presentation

### The alphabet

**Capital letters:**  A  B  C  D  E  F  G  H  I  J  K  L  M
N  O  P  Q  R  S  T  U  V  W  X  Y  Z

**Small letters:**  a  b  c  d  e  f  g  h  i  j  k  l  m
n  o  p  q  r  s  t  u  v  w  x  y  z

### Asking for spelling and pronunciation

A: How do you spell Winfield?
B: Capital W -i -n -f -i -e -l -d.

If you see a new word, ask:
How do you pronounce this word?

# UNIT 3

**COMMUNICATION**
Making a telephone call • Asking for and giving location • Talking about names, addresses, and phone numbers

**PRACTICAL LANGUAGE**
More classroom instructions • Days, months

**GRAMMAR**
*Be*: yes/no questions, short answers • *Who, what, where* questions • Prepositions: *at* + place; *at* + home/work/ school; *in* + room

## Is Bob There?

*Mike Young is a student at Winfield High School. Mike is calling his friend, Bob Logan. Bob's brother, Sam, answers the telephone.*

SAM:   Hello.
MIKE:  Hello, Bob?
SAM:   No. This is Sam.
MIKE:  Oh, hi, Sam. It's Mike.
SAM:   Oh, hi, Mike.
MIKE:  Is Bob there?
SAM:   I'm not sure. Just a minute.

SAM:   Hey, Mom.
      Where's Bob?
ADELA: He's in his room.

SAM:   Bob. Phone. It's Mike.
BOB:   OK. Coming.
     . . .
SAM:   Hi, Mike? He's coming.
MIKE:  Thanks, Sam.

## 1 Presentation

### Asking for and giving location

| Say: | at home | BUT | at the garage |
|---|---|---|---|
| | at work | | at the hospital |
| | at school | | at the office |

**A**

A: Where's Adela?
B: She's at home.

**B**

A: Where are Ted and Howard?
B: They're at home.

**C**

A: Where's Sam?
B: He's at work.
   He's at the garage.

**D**

A: Where's Elinor?
B: She's at work.
   She's at the hospital.

**E**

A: Where's Tom?
B: He's at work.
   He's at the office.

**F**

A: Where's Liz?
B: She's at work. She's at
   the telephone company.

**G**

A: Where are Bob and Mike?
B: They're at school.

**H**

A: Where are Lisa and Joyce?
B: They're at school.

## 2 Pronunciation

**Repeat the question and the phrases.**

Where's Sam?

at home      at the office      at the telephone company

at work      at the hospital

at school      at the garage

## 3 Practice

It's Monday afternoon. Practice asking and answering questions about where the people are in the pictures in *1*.

## 4 Presentation 🔊

**Asking for someone on the phone**

A

> Dr. = Doctor

MAN:      Is Dr. Young there?
HOWARD: No, she isn't. She's at the hospital.
MAN:      OK. I'll call later.

B

WOMAN: Is Ted Young there?
HOWARD: Yes, he is. Just a minute.
WOMAN: OK.
HOWARD: Ted. Phone.

C

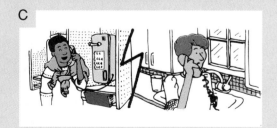

SEKILA: Is Sam there?
ADELA: No, he isn't. He's at work.
SEKILA: Thank you. I'll call later.

## 5 Interaction

Write the names of two family members on a piece of paper. Exchange papers with a partner. Call your friend's house and ask for the people.

> A: Hello.
> B: Hello. This is _____ . Is _____ there?
> A: No, _____ .
> _____ at _____ .
> B: _____ . I'll call later.

## 6 Vocabulary in Context

Places in and around the home

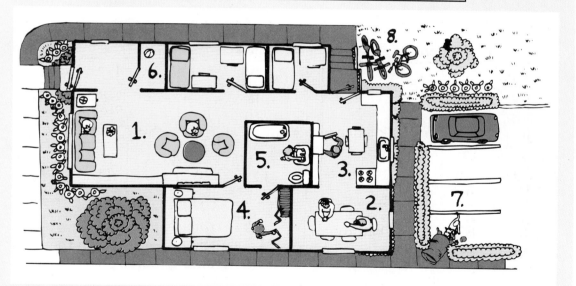

Use **in + the + room**, **closet**, **yard**, **parking lot**.

1. The cats, Duchess and Princess, are in the **living room**.
2. Bob and Sam are in the **dining room**.
3. Tom's in the **kitchen**.
4. Adela's in the **bedroom**.
5. Lisa's in the **bathroom**.
6. The basketball is in the **closet**.
7. The dog (Superman) and the car are in the **parking lot**.
8. The bikes are in the **yard**.

## 7 Practice

Look at the picture on page 27. It's Saturday. The Logans and their pets are all at home. Ask and answer questions about where they are.

> Tom
> A:  Where's Tom?
> B:  He's in the kitchen.

| | |
|---|---|
| **1.** Lisa | **5.** the bicycles |
| **2.** Bob and Sam | **6.** the car |
| **3.** Duchess and Princess (the cats) | **7.** Superman (the dog) |
| **4.** Adela | **8.** Bob |

## 8 Presentation

### Asking about location

Yes/No Questions

| Am | I | |
|---|---|---|
| Is | he<br>she<br>it | in the kitchen? |
| Are | we<br>you<br>they | |

Short Answers

| | | |
|---|---|---|
| | I | am. |
| Yes, | he<br>she<br>it | is. |
| | we<br>you<br>they | are. |

| | | |
|---|---|---|
| | I | 'm not. |
| No, | he<br>she<br>it | isn't. |
| | we<br>you<br>they | aren't. |

**A**
> A:  Is Lisa in the bathroom?
> B:  Yes, she is.

**B**
> A:  Is Bob in the bedroom?
> B:  No, he isn't.  He's in the dining room.

**C**
> A:  Are the bikes in the yard?
> B:  Yes, they are.

**D**
> A:  Are the cats in the kitchen?
> B:  No, they aren't.  They're in the living room.

## 9 Practice

**Ask and answer questions about people and things in the apartment. Follow the conversation models in 8.**

1. Lisa / bedroom
2. cats / living room
3. Tom / bathroom
4. basketball / closet
5. Adela / dining room

6. bikes / parking lot
7. Superman / yard
8. Bob and Sam / living room
9. Adela / bedroom
10. basketball / parking lot

## 10 Presentation

**Correcting a statement**

| (am not) | I'm not. |
|---|---|
| (is not) | He's not.<br>She's not.<br>It's not. |
| (are not) | We're not.<br>You're not.<br>They're not. |

Look at the drawing of the Logans' apartment on page 27.

**A**
A: Where's Sam?
B: He's in the kitchen.
C: No, he's not.
    He's in the dining room.
B: Oh, you're right.

**B**
A: Where are the cats?
B: They're in the yard.
C: No, they're not.
    They're in the living room.
B: Oh, you're right.

## 11 Practice

**Look at the diagram of the Logans' apartment on page 27. Make an incorrect statement. Another student will correct your statement.**

## 12 Presentation

### Asking about people, pets, and things

A
> A: Who's in the kitchen?
> B: Tom is.

B
> A: Who's in the living room?
> B: The cats are.

C
> A: What's in the parking lot?
> B: The car is.

D
> A: What's in the yard?
> B: The bikes are.

## 13 Practice

Work with a partner. Ask about people, pets, and things in the Logans' apartment. Follow the conversation models in 12.

## 14 Presentation

### Saying a telephone number

| | |
|---|---|
| Mom | 659-4550 |
| Dad | 659-1272 |
| Gloria | 659-0883 |
| Sam | 659-1124 |
| Tino | 659-3578 |
| Cristina | 659-1833 |
| Ann | 657-3060 |
| Dave | 659-3345 |
| Sue | 659-0034 |
| Meiling | 657-1225 |
| | |
| | |

1. Gloria's number is
   six-five-nine, oh-eight-eight-three.
2. My mom's number is
   six-five-nine, four-five-five-oh.
3. My dad's number is
   six-five-nine, one-two-seven-two.

## 15 Practice

Practice with a partner.  Ask for a telephone number from Liz's book.  Follow the conversation model in *14*.

## 16 Listening

Number your paper from 1-8.  Listen and write the telephone number in each conversation.

| | |
|---|---|
| YOU HEAR: | What's your telephone number? |
| | Five-four-seven, one-nine-two-three. |
| WRITE: | 547-1923 |

### Giving information about name and address

**1.** This is Mike Young.

New York State Department of Health
*Certificate of Birth Registration*
This certifies that a certificate of birth has been filed under the name of:
Michael Stuart Young

*Sex:* Male

*Born on:* June 1, 1972, at 7:26 AM

*At:* Winfield Hospital , New York
Winfield
*Name of father:* Howard S. Young

*Maiden name of mother:* Elinor E. Adams

*Date filed:* June 8, 1972      *Local Registration No.:* 1149

*Date issued:* June 8, 1972

John Evans
Registrar of Vital Statistics
*Address:* Winfield, New York
This notice is void if it contains any erasures or corrections.

**2.** This is his birth certificate.
**3.** His **full name** is Michael Stuart Young.
**4.** His **last name** is Young.
**5.** His **first name** is Michael, but his **nickname** is Mike.
**6.** His **middle name** is Stuart.
**7.** His **middle initial** is S.

| | |
|---|---|
| SECRETARY: | Full name, please? |
| MIKE: | Michael Stuart Young. |
| SECRETARY: | What's your address? |
| MIKE: | 10 South Kennedy Avenue Winfield, New York |
| SECRETARY: | Zip code? |
| MIKE: | 11500 |

**Other addresses:**

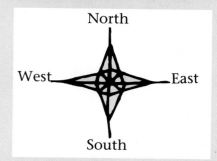

**Abbreviations:**
St. = Street
Rd. = Road
Blvd. = Boulevard
Ave. = Avenue

Jennifer King
627 N. Prince St.
Winfield, New York  11500

Charles Grant
2105 E. Park Rd.
Winfield, New York  11500

Nancy Mann
3311 W. Benson Blvd.
Winfield, New York  11500

Antonio Mendes
19 Eagle St.
Winfield, New York  11500

## 18 Writing

**Copy the registration card neatly and complete it with your name, address, and telephone number.**

Please print all information.

Class: _____   Teacher: _____

Name: _____
         (Last)        (First)      (Middle Initial)
Address: _____
              (Street)
         _____
              (City)           (State)        (Zip)
Telephone: _____   Sex:   M   F

## 19 Practice

**Now, answer your partner's questions.**

1. What's your name?
2. How do you spell that, please?
3. What's your address?
4. Your telephone number, please?

# Practical Language

## 1 Presentation

### More classroom instructions

1. Sit with a partner.
2. Form a group of three.
3. Stand up and move to your group.
4. Sit down, please.
5. Come to the board, please.
6. Point to the book.
7. Read this sentence out loud.
8. Write these words.

## 2 Presentation and Practice

### The days of the week and months of the year

| Days | Months | |
|---|---|---|
| Sunday | January (Jan.) | July |
| Monday | February (Feb.) | August (Aug.) |
| Tuesday | March (Mar.) | September (Sept.) |
| Wednesday | April (Apr.) | October (Oct.) |
| Thursday | May | November (Nov.) |
| Friday | June | December (Dec.) |
| Saturday | | |

Say a day or a month.  Your partner will say the next day or month.

> A: Thursday
> B: Friday
> A: How do you spell Friday?
> B: Capital F - r - i - d - a - y.

# UNIT 4

COMMUNICATION
Talking about people's activities ▪
Making and responding to suggestions ▪
Making excuses ▪ Making plans
PRACTICAL LANGUAGE
Telling time

GRAMMAR
Present continuous: affirmative and negative
statements, yes/no questions, short answers,
questions with *what* ▪ *Be* + adjective ▪
*Let's* + verb ▪ *Have to* + verb

# Let's Do Something

*It's Saturday afternoon.  Bob is at Mike's house.*

MIKE:  C'mon Bob.  Let's do something.  It's a beautiful afternoon.
BOB:  Yeah. You're right.
MIKE:  Let's play baseball.  What's Sam doing?
BOB:  He's busy.  He's studying for an exam.
MIKE:  Oh, too bad.

*A few minutes later.*
MIKE:  Hey, look.  There's Gloria.
       She's going to the tennis courts.
BOB:  Yeah ... Hey, Mike, let's play
       tennis instead.
MIKE:  Great idea!  Let's go.
BOB:  I have to get my racquet.
MIKE:  OK. Meet you at the courts.

### Describing actions in progress

> Use present continuous to
> describe actions in progress.

**Present Continuous**

**Affirmative Statements**

| I'm | |
|---|---|
| He's / She's | working. |
| We're / You're / They're | |

**Negative Statements**

| I | 'm not | |
|---|---|---|
| He / She | isn't | studying. |
| We / You / They | aren't | |

A

A: Is Liz busy?
B: Yes, she is.  She's fixing
   the car.

B

A: Is Bob busy?
B: Yes, he is.  He's cleaning
   the kitchen.

C

A: Are Lisa and Joyce busy?
B: Yes, they are.  They're washing
   the dog.

D

A: Is Cristina busy?
B: Yes, she is.  She's calling Gino.

E

A: Is Adela busy?
B: Yes, she is.  She's painting the bathroom.

F

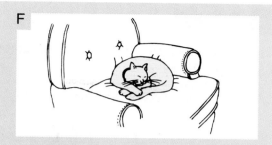

The cat, Duchess, isn't busy.
She's sleeping.

G

The Youngs aren't busy.
They're relaxing.
They're reading the newspaper.

H

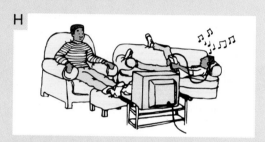

Ted and Mike aren't busy.
They're relaxing.
Ted's listening to music.
Mike is watching TV.

## 2 Pronunciation

**Repeat these sentences.**

1.  He's watching TV.
2.  She's painting the bathroom.

3.  He's cleaning the kitchen.
4.  They're listening to music.

## 3 Practice

**Work with a partner.  Ask and answer questions about the people and Duchess in 1.  Follow the conversation models.**

## 4 Practice

Make incorrect statements about the pictures on pages 36-37. Another student will correct you.

> A: Ted is watching TV.
> B: No, he isn't watching TV. He's listening to music.
> A: Oh, you're right.

> A: The Youngs are working.
> B: No, they aren't working. They're relaxing.
> A: Oh, you're right.

## 5 Listening

Number your paper from 1-10. Listen to the description and write the letter of the picture on pages 36-37.

> YOU HEAR: They're reading the newspaper.
> WRITE: <u>G</u>

## 6 Presentation

### Asking and answering questions about people's activities

**Present Continuous**

**Yes/No Questions**

| Am | I | |
|---|---|---|
| Is | he she | working? |
| Are | we you they | |

**Short Answers**

| | I | am. |
|---|---|---|
| Yes, | he she | is. |
| | we you they | are. |

| | I | 'm not. |
|---|---|---|
| No, | he she | isn't. |
| | we you they | aren't. |

**Look at the pictures on pages 36-37.**

A

A: Is Bob studying?
B: No, he isn't. He's cleaning the kitchen.

B

A: Are Joyce and Lisa washing the car?
B: No, they aren't. They're washing Superman.

## 7 Practice

**Ask and answer questions about the pictures on pages 36-37.**

1. Liz / fix the car
2. Bob / clean his room
3. Ted and Mike / study
4. Adela / clean the bathroom
5. Joyce and Lisa / listen to music
6. the cat / sleep
7. Howard / read a book
8. Cristina / call her mother
9. Elinor and Howard / read the newspaper
10. Mike / study

## 8 Presentation

**Asking what people are doing**

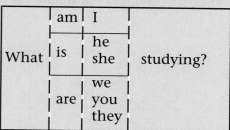

**Information Questions: *What***

| What | am | I | studying? |
|------|-----|-----|-----------|
|  | is | he | |
|  |  | she | |
|  | are | we | |
|  |  | you | |
|  |  | they | |

A

A: What's Cristina doing?
B: She's calling Gino.

B

A: What are Lisa and Joyce doing?
B: They're washing the dog.

C

CRISTINA: Hi, Gino. This is Cris. Are you busy?
GINO: No, I'm not. I'm watching TV.

D

MIKE: Hi, Bob. This is Mike. Are you busy?
BOB: Yes, I am.
MIKE: What are you doing?
BOB: I'm studying.

## 9 Practice

Practice with a partner. Take turns asking and answering questions about what the people are doing in the pictures on pages 36-37. Follow conversation models A and B in *8*.

## 10 Interaction

Work with a partner. Call and find out what he or she is doing.

A: Hello.
B: Hi, _____ . This is _____ .
   How are you?
A: _____ . And you?
B: _____ . Are you busy?

A: Yes, I am.
B: What are you doing?
A: I'm _____ .

A: No, I'm not.
   I'm _____ .

## Making and responding to suggestions

Use **let's** + *verb* to make a suggestion.
Use **have to** + *verb* when giving an excuse.

let's = let us

A
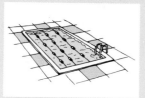
the pool

B

the zoo

C

the park

D

the | movies
movie theater

E

the basketball court

**Pronunciation:**
•
have to / hæftə /

c'mon = come on

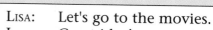

F

BOB: C'mon, Sam. Let's play basketball.
SAM: Sorry. I have to study.
BOB: Too bad. Well... see you later.
SAM: Yeah. See you later.

G

LISA: Let's go to the movies.
JOYCE: Great idea!
LISA: Meet you at the movie theater in 10 minutes.
JOYCE: OK.

## 12 Practice

**Work with a partner. Practice making suggestions and responding politely. Use conversations F and G in _11_ as models.**

1. pool / sorry / study
2. play tennis / great / court / in 15 minutes
3. zoo / sorry / do my homework
4. movies / great / theater / in 20 minutes
5. park / sorry / babysit
6. pool / sorry / clean the apartment
7. movies / sorry / babysit
8. play basketball / great /court / in 10 minutes
9. park / sorry / clean the yard
10. pool / great / pool / in 15 minutes

> **Useful vocabulary:**
>
> do my homework = study
>
> babysit
>

## 13 Interaction

**Work with your teacher and classmates and list ten or more places to go in your city. Then work with a classmate. Your classmate is at your house. You aren't busy. Suggest an activity. Your classmate can accept or refuse. Complete the conversation and role play it for the class.**

> A: C'mon _____ . Let's _____ .

**Accept**

> B: That's a good idea.
>    Meet you at _____ in ____ minutes.
> A: OK.

**Refuse**

> B: Sorry. I have to _____ .
> A: Too bad. See you _____ .
> B: Yeah. See you _____ .

## 14 Reading

### Before You Read

1. Do you write notes to your friends?
2. Do you suggest activities in your notes?

Gloria,
Let's play tennis today after school. Let's meet in the parking lot at 3:00.
Bob

Bob,
great idea! No problem but let's meet at my place at 3:30. OK? See you then.
Gloria

### After You Read

**Read the statement. Say *That's right* or *That's wrong*.**

1. Bob is playing tennis now.
2. Gloria is busy this afternoon.
3. Bob and Gloria are at school.
4. at my place =
   a. at the park
   b. at school
   c. at my home

## 15 Writing

A. **Rewrite these notes correctly. You have to change some small letters to capital letters. Put periods at the end of sentences.**

joyce,
    let's go to the pool
friday afternoon let's
meet at the pool at
2:00 see you there
                lisa

lisa,
    i'm busy friday
let's go saturday
let's meet at my
house at 10:00
                joyce

B. **Now complete Lisa's answer to Joyce.**

_____,
    OK. I'll _____ you at
your _____ at _____
on _____.
                _____

# Practical Language

## 1 Presentation

### Telling time

A

What time is it?
It's twelve o'clock.

B

It's four o'clock.

C

It's six ten.
It's ten after six.

D

It's seven fifteen.

E

It's eight twenty.
It's twenty after eight.

F

It's nine thirty.

G

It's ten forty-five.

H

It's eleven fifty-five.
It's five to twelve.

## 2 Practice

**Practice with a partner. Take turns asking what time it is.**

1.

2.

3.

4.

5.

6.

## 3 Presentation

### Asking for the time

A: Excuse me. What time is it?

B: It's twelve o'clock.
A: Thank you.
Thanks.

B: Sorry. I don't have a watch.
A: OK. Thanks anyway.

COMMUNICATION
Ending a conversation ▪ Talking about
nationality ▪ Talking about ability
PRACTICAL LANGUAGE
Ordinal numbers ▪ Dates

GRAMMAR
*Can/can't* + verb:  affirmative and negative
statements, yes/no questions, short
answers ▪ Coordination: *but*

# Can You Speak Another Language?

*Bob Logan sits down next to Gloria Rivera in the Winfield High School cafeteria.*
*Gloria is reading a letter.  She looks up and sees Bob.*

GLORIA:  Hi, Bob.  How's everything?

BOB:  Fine.  How are you doing?

GLORIA:  Great!  My cousin's coming to visit from Puerto Rico.

BOB:  That's nice. ...  Oh, that's right.  You're Puerto Rican.

GLORIA:  Not exactly.  My parents are from Puerto Rico, but I was born
in New York.

BOB:  Can you speak Spanish?

GLORIA:  Sure.  We speak Spanish at home.  How about you?  Can you speak
another language?

BOB:  I can speak Spanish, but not very well.

GLORIA:  Maybe I can help you.  . . . What time is it, Bob?

BOB:  12:25.

GLORIA:  Oh no!  Excuse me.  I have to go.  I have a class at 12:30.
See you later.

BOB:  OK.  Bye.

**Presentation** 🔲

### Ending a conversation

> GLORIA: What time is it, Mike?
> MIKE: 2:15.
> GLORIA: Oh no! Excuse me. I have to go. I have a doctor's appointment at 2:30.
> MIKE: OK. See you later.

2 **Interaction**

**Complete the conversation, practice it, and role play it for the class.**

**Useful vocabulary:**
dentist appointment
exam
class

> A: What time is it, _____ ?
> B: _____ .
> A: Oh no! Excuse me. I have to go.
>    I have | a   | _____ at _____ .
>            | an  |
> B: OK. See you _____ .

### Talking about nationality and language ability

|  | | |
|---|---|---|
| I | | |
| You | can | |
| He | can't | speak English. |
| She | (cannot) | |
| We | | |
| They | | |

| Country | Nationality | Language |
|---|---|---|
| Brazil | Brazilian | Portuguese |
| Colombia | Colombian | Spanish |
| the Soviet Union | Soviet/Russian | Russian |
| Italy | Italian | Italian |
| Korea | Korean | Korean |
| Mexico | Mexican | Spanish |
| the United States | American | English |
| China | Chinese | Chinese |
| Japan | Japanese | Japanese |
| Vietnam | Vietnamese | Vietnamese |
| France | French | French |

A

Nhu Trinh is Vietnamese.
She's from Vietnam originally.
She can speak Vietnamese and
English.
She can speak a little Portuguese,
but not very well.

B

Carlos and Ana Nava are from
Mexico.
They are Mexican.
They can speak Spanish and
English.
They can't speak Japanese.

Listen and compare.   Then repeat the sentences.

| Not emphasized | Emphasized |
|---|---|
| / kən / | / kænt / |

1. I can speak Spanish.
2. He can speak Russian.
3. They can speak French.

I can't speak Chinese.
He can't speak Italian.
They can't speak Korean.

**5** Practice

Talk about the language ability of the *Intercom 2000* characters.

> Carlos  / Mexican // Spanish / Russian
> Carlos is Mexican.
> He can speak Spanish.  He can't speak Russian.

1. Gino  / Italian // Italian / Japanese
2. Tom Logan / American // English / Spanish
3. Howard and Elinor /American // English / French
4. Nhu Trinh / Vietnamese // Vietnamese / Chinese
5. Cristina / Colombian // Spanish and English / Portuguese
6. Toshio Ito  / Japanese // Japanese and English  / Italian
7. Liz and Lisa /American // English / Vietnamese
8. Mike / American // English / Russian
9. Lisa / American // English / Korean
10. Carlos and Ana / Mexican // Spanish and English / French

**6** Practice

Tell your classmates about your language ability.

> I'm from _____ .
> I can speak _____ .
> We speak _____ at home.
> I can speak _____ , but not very well.
> I can speak a little _____ .
> I can't speak _____ .

## 7 Vocabulary in Context

### Artistic and athletic talents

**A**

Sam can ride a bike.
Bob can run fast.

**B**

Liz can't ski.

**C**

Joyce can draw.

**Other games:**

football    baseball

volleyball    soccer

**D**

Mike can roller skate,
but not very well.

**E**

Bob and Mike can play
basketball.

**F**

Lisa can sing.

**G**

Cristina and Gino can
dance.

**H**

Lisa can't drive.

**Other instruments:**

violin    piano

drums    clarinet

**I**

Ted can swim, but not
very well.

**J**

Gloria can play the
guitar.

## 8 Practice

**Tell the class something about what you can and can't do.**

> I can sing, but I can't draw.
> I can play the guitar, but not very well.

## 9 Presentation

### Asking about ability

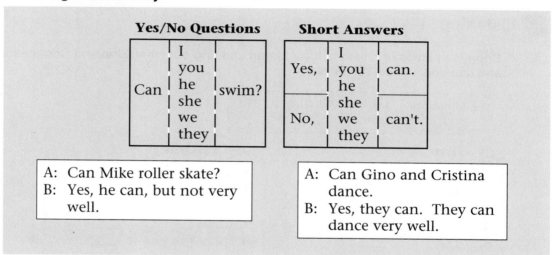

**Yes/No Questions**

| Can | I<br>you<br>he<br>she<br>we<br>they | swim? |

**Short Answers**

| Yes, | I<br>you<br>he | can. |
| No, | she<br>we<br>they | can't. |

A: Can Mike roller skate?
B: Yes, he can, but not very well.

A: Can Gino and Cristina dance.
B: Yes, they can. They can dance very well.

## 10 Pronunciation

**Listen and compare. Then repeat the sentences.**

| Not emphasized | Emphasized |
|---|---|
| / kən / | / kæn / or /kænt / |

1. Can you sing?
2. Can he ski?
3. Can she dance?
4. Can they play the piano?

Yes, I can.
No, I can't.
No, he can't.
Yes, she can.
No, they can't.

## 11 Practice

**Work with a partner. Ask and answer questions about the abilities of the *Intercom 2000* characters.**

1. Sam / ride a bike
2. Liz / ski
3. Bob / run fast
4. Mike / roller skate
5. Lisa / sing

6. Lisa / drive
7. Bob and Mike / play basketball
8. Gloria / play the guitar
9. Ted / swim
10. Cristina and Gino / dance

## 12 Listening

**Copy the names and lists below. Listen and find out what Gino and Cristina can and can't do. Write *Yes* or *No*.**

| | |
|---|---|
| YOU HEAR: | Gino can't play tennis. |
| WRITE: | tennis __No__ |

### Gino

1. sing _____
2. play soccer _____
3. drive _____
4. swim _____
5. draw _____

### Cristina

6. ski _____
7. drive _____
8. swim _____
9. draw _____
10. play the guitar _____

## 13 Reading

### Before You Read

1. What is the Queen of England's name?
2. Who are her children? Are they married?
3. Look at the caption under the first picture. Who is this famous person?
4. Look at the caption under the second picture. What can this person do? What is her husband's name?

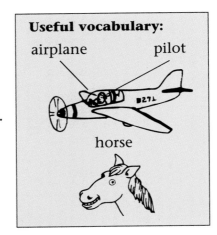

**Useful vocabulary:**

airplane   pilot

horse

# Fergie in New York

**THE DUCHESS OF YORK:**
*Sarah Ferguson: beautiful and friendly*

NEW YORK — The Duchess of York, Sarah Ferguson, is visiting New York. Sarah's nickname is Fergie. She is a beautiful and talented woman. People like her because she is friendly.

Fergie's husband, Prince Andrew, is a navy pilot. Fergie can fly a plane, too. She is also athletic. She rides horses, and she can ski and swim.

The Duchess arrives at Kennedy Airport this morning. She is going to the Statue of Liberty and Chinatown. On Thursday she is going to a Broadway musical. Fergie is excited about her trip to New York!

**SHE CAN FLY:**
*Sarah flies planes and helicopters. Her husband, Prince Andrew, is a pilot, too.*

## After You Read

**Complete the sentences and answer the questions.**

1. Sarah Ferguson is the _____ of York.
2. Her _____ is Prince Andrew, the son of Queen Elizabeth of England.
3. Sarah's nickname is _____ .
4. She can fly a plane. What else can she do? (Name three things.)

## 14 Listening

Listen and copy the correct words on your paper.

**Corena Harwell**

1. Canadian / American
2. English / Korean
3. swim / run fast / draw

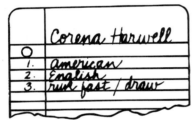

Corena Harwell
1. american
2. English
3. run fast / draw

A

**Leon Pinson**

1. American / Brazilian
2. Spanish / English
3. sing / play the guitar / play soccer

B

**Scott Miller**

1. Canadian / American
2. French / English
3. play baseball / ski / play the violin

C

**Sasha Danilov**

1. Italian / Russian
2. Russian / English
3. draw / dance / swim

## 15 Writing

Use the pictures above or bring pictures of famous people to class. Write the answers to these questions for each picture.

- Who's in the picture?
- What nationality is he/she?
- What language(s) can he/she speak?
- What can he/she do?

This is Stevie Wonder. He's American. He can speak English. He can play the piano. He can sing.

# Practical Language

## 1 Presentation

### Ordinal numbers and dates

| | | | | | |
|---|---|---|---|---|---|
| **1st** | first | **11th** | eleventh | **21st** | twenty-first |
| **2nd** | second | **12th** | twelfth | **22nd** | twenty-second |
| **3rd** | third | **13th** | thirteenth | **23rd** | twenty-third |
| **4th** | fourth | **14th** | fourteenth | **24th** | twenty-fourth |
| **5th** | fifth | **15th** | fifteenth | **25th** | twenty-fifth |
| **6th** | sixth | **16th** | sixteenth | **26th** | twenty-sixth |
| **7th** | seventh | **17th** | seventeenth | **27th** | twenty-seventh |
| **8th** | eighth | **18th** | eighteenth | **28th** | twenty-eighth |
| **9th** | ninth | **19th** | nineteenth | **29th** | twenty-ninth |
| **10th** | tenth | **20th** | twentieth | **30th** | thirtieth |
| | | | | **31st** | thirty-first |

### Saying the date

Say:  Monday, September tenth, nineteen ninety
We can write it:  9/10/90

## 2 Practice

### A. Say each day and date.

**1.** Wednesday, March 11, 1970
**2.** Monday, August 30, 1943
**3.** Friday, May 5, 1950
**4.** Monday, June 18, 1979
**5.** Saturday, February 3, 1991
**6.** Thursday, December 5, 1963
**7.** Tuesday, September 25, 1945
**8.** Sunday, January 1, 1905
**9.** Saturday, July 27, 1985
**10.** Friday, April 13, 1990

### B. Write the dates with numbers.

March 11, 1970
3/11/70

COMMUNICATION
Talking about the location and size of cities • Asking about place of origin • Locating places on streets • Asking about destination • Inviting someone to come along

PRACTICAL LANGUAGE
Asking for help • Responding when you don't know or can't remember

GRAMMAR
Prepositions: *in* + city, state, country; *near* + place; *on* + street name • *Be* + adjective • Intensifier *very* + adjective

# What's Winfield Like?

*Gloria Rivera is in New York City. She is visiting her old school. It's 3:30 and school is out for the day. She's talking with her friend, Janet Levin.*

JANET:    Where are you going now, Gloria?
GLORIA:  To the post office. What about you?
JANET:    Home, but let's get a soda first.
GLORIA:  Good idea.

JANET:    What's Winfield like, Gloria?
GLORIA:  It's small, but it has everything — a lot of nice stores and a community college.
JANET:    Is it pretty?
GLORIA:  Yes, it is. It's on a bay. It has a nice marina. Why don't you come for a visit?
JANET:    That's a great idea!

# 1 Presentation

## Asking about the location and size of cities

**A**

A: Where's Houston?
B: It's **in** Texas.
A: Is it big?
B: Yes. It's very big.

**B**

A: Where's Baytown?
B: It's **near** Houston.
A: Is it big?
B: No. It's small.
It's not very big.

# 2 Pronunciation

**Repeat these questions.**

1. Where's Los Angeles?

2. Where's Paris?

3. Where are you from?

4. Is it big?

5. Is it pretty?

6. Is it nice?

Repeat the names of the cities and states after your teacher. Locate the cities on the map and find out which states they are in. Match the city with its state.

> San Francisco is in California.

| Cities | | States |
|---|---|---|
| **1.** San Francisco | **9.** Lynn | **a.** Louisiana |
| **2.** Houston | **10.** Seattle | **b.** New York |
| **3.** Baytown | **11.** Tacoma | **c.** Florida |
| **4.** Chicago | **12.** Miami | **d.** California |
| **5.** Elgin | **13.** New Orleans | **e.** Washington |
| **6.** St. Louis | **14.** New York City | **f.** Illinois |
| **7.** Los Angeles | **15.** Arlington | **g.** Virginia |
| **8.** Boston | | **h.** Missouri |
| | | **i.** Massachusetts |
| | | **j.** Texas |

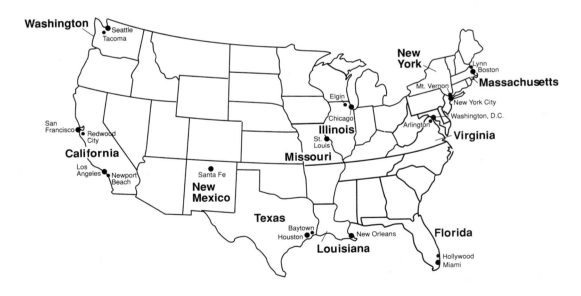

**4** Practice

Work with a partner. Ask about the location and size of cities on the map. Follow the conversation models in *1*.

## 5 Practice

Work as a class. Make a list of big and small cities that you know. Ask and answer questions about their location and size.

> A: Paris.
> B: Where's Paris?
> A: It's in France.
> B: Is it big?
> A: It's very big.

## 6 Presentation

**Asking about place of origin or hometown**

> A: Where are you from?
> B: Tacoma.
> A: Where's that?
> B: Near Seattle, Washington.
> A: What's it like?
> B: It's small, but nice.

## 7 Interaction

Pretend you are at a party. You are talking to someone new. Practice this conversation with a partner.

> A: Where are you from?
> B: I'm from _____ .
> A: Where's that?
> B: It's _____ .
> A: What's it like?
> B: It's _____ .

## 8 Presentation

### Locating places in a city

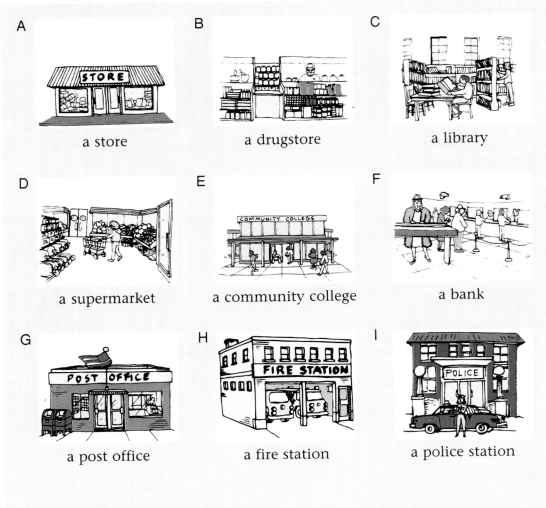

A  a store

B  a drugstore

C  a library

D  a supermarket

E  a community college

F  a bank

G  a post office

H  a fire station

I  a police station

J
A: Where's the bookstore?
B: It's right here.

K
A: Where are the schools?
B: Here's one.
C: Here's another.

**Store** is a general word.
A **bookstore** sells **books**.
A **candy store** sells **candy**.

## 9 Practice

Work with a partner. Take turns asking about these places on the map of Winfield. Use the conversation models in *8*.

1. marina
2. hotels
3. train station
4. bus station
5. zoo

6. churches
7. city hall
8. park
9. pool
10. movie theaters

11. restaurants
12. museum
13. Community College
14. library
15. schools

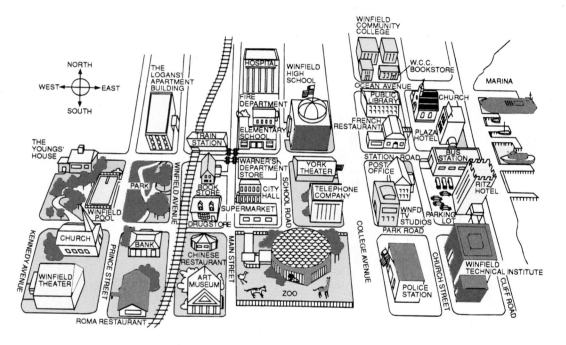

## 10 Presentation

### Locating places on streets

A
| | |
|---|---|
| A: | Where's Kennedy Avenue? |
| B: | It's right here. |

B
| | |
|---|---|
| A: | What's **on** Kennedy Avenue? |
| B: | The Winfield Theater. |

C
| | |
|---|---|
| A: | Where's the Roma Restaurant? |
| B: | It's **on** Prince Street. |

## 11 Practice

**Work with a partner. Locate these streets on the map of Winfield on page 61. Talk about what's on each street. Follow conversation models A and B in *10*.**

1. Kennedy Avenue
2. Winfield Avenue
3. Ocean Avenue
4. Prince Street
5. Main Street
6. College Avenue
7. Church Street
8. School Road
9. Cliff Road
10. Station Road

## 12 Practice

**Work with a partner. Take turns asking for the location of these places. Follow conversation model C in *10*.**

1. hospital
2. telephone company
3. post office
4. library
5. bank
6. zoo
7. Chinese restaurant
8. York Theater
9. college bookstore
10. elementary school

## 13 Listening

**Number your paper from 1-10. Look at the map of Winfield. Listen to each sentence and write *Yes* or *No*.**

| | |
|---|---|
| YOU HEAR: | The bus station is on Station Road. |
| WRITE: | Yes |

## 14 Presentation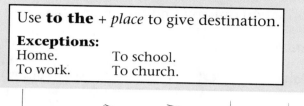

**Asking about destination; inviting someone to come along**

Use **to the** + *place* to give destination.
**Exceptions:**
Home.          To school.
To work.       To church.

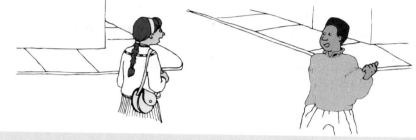

GLORIA: Where are you going?
MIKE:    To the post office.
GLORIA: Where's that?
MIKE:    It's on Church Street.  Why don't you come along?
GLORIA: OK.

## 15 Practice

Pretend you are new in Winfield.  You meet a friend.  Find out where he or she is going.  He or she will suggest that you come along.  Use the conversation model in *14*.

1. train station / Main Street
2. bus station / Station Road
3. French restaurant / Church Street
4. Roma / Prince Street
5. museum / Main Street
6. Winfield Theater / Kennedy Avenue
7. community college / College Avenue
8. bank / Park Road
9. Chinese restaurant / Main Street
10. police station / College Avenue

## 16 Reading

### Before You Read

What information can you find on a map?

### Things You Need to Know

1. Los Angeles is a very big city. It has small cities in it.
2. Santa Monica, Bel Air, Hollywood, and Beverly Hills are small cities in greater Los Angeles.
3. This map of Los Angeles shows the big streets and the location of hotels.
4. Coliseums and stadiums usually look like this. ──── They are usually for sports events.

# Los Angeles

3 days from $79 to $189 plus airfare.
Including half-day city tour.

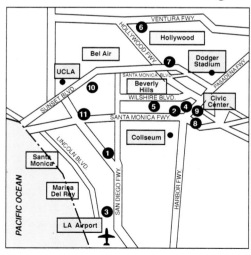

|  | DOUBLE | | SINGLE | |
|---|---|---|---|---|
|  | 2 Nights | Extra Night | 2 Nights | Extra Night |
| ① Holiday Inn Airport | $79 | $40 | $40 | $40 |
| ② Figueroa | 95 | 37 | 37 | 37 |
| ③ Los Angeles Airport Hilton | 99 | 50 | 50 | 50 |
| ④ Mayfair Hotel | 105 | 42 | 42 | 42 |
| ⑤ Hyatt Wilshire | 119 | 49 | 49 | 49 |
| ⑥ Holiday Inn Hollywood | 119 | 49 | 49 | 49 |
| ⑦ Hyatt on Sunset | 125 | 52 | 52 | 52 |
| ⑧ Bonaventure | 145 | 62 | 62 | 62 |
| ⑨ Biltmore Hotel | 175 | 77 | 77 | 77 |
| ⑩ Beverly Hilton | 185 | 82 | 82 | 82 |
| ⑪ Century Plaza | 185 | 84 | 84 | 84 |

**After You Read**

**A. Look at the map.** Say *That's right, That's wrong,* or *I don't know.*

1. Dodger Stadium is near the ocean.
2. Santa Monica has a beach.
3. The University of California at Los Angeles (UCLA) is near Marina del Rey.
4. Santa Monica Boulevard is on the map.
5. The Beverly Hilton is in Hollywood.

**B. Answer these questions about the map.**

1. You are going to Los Angeles. You want a hotel near the Coliseum. What hotels are near the Coliseum?
2. You have friends in Marina del Rey. What hotel is near their house?
3. What street is the Hyatt Wilshire on?

## 17 Writing

Copy the sentences in a paragraph. Indent the first sentence. (See the example.) Capitalize the first word of every sentence and the names of cities, states, and countries. Put a period at the end of each sentence.

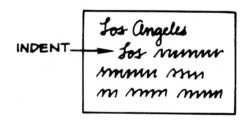

INDENT

1. los angeles is a city in california

2. california is a state in the united states of america

3. california is on the pacific ocean

4. los angeles is a very big city

5. hollywood and beverly hills are small cities in greater los angeles

# Practical Language

## 1 Presentation

### Asking for help in your English class

1. I don't understand. Please speak more slowly.
2. Can I borrow a pen?
3. Can I have a piece of paper?

### Asking for information in your English class

1. A: What does __town__ mean?
   B: It means __small city__ .

2. A: How do you say _____ in English?
   B: _____

3. A: How do you pronounce this word?
   B: _____

## 2 Presentation

### Responding when you don't know or you can't remember

1. A: Who's this?
   B: I don't know.

2. A: What's this?
   B: I'm sorry. I can't remember.

COMMUNICATION
Shopping in a supermarket ▪ Talking about location ▪ Thanking and responding to thanks ▪ Expressing quantity ▪ Asking for a favor

GRAMMAR
Countable vs. noncountable nouns ▪ Prepositions: *next to, across from* ▪ Expressions of quantity: *a . . . of* ▪ *Can* in requests

# We Need Some Things from the Supermarket

*Adela Logan is a busy woman. She's a homemaker. She's also studying computer programming at the Winfield Technical Institute. She's at home right now. She has a big test in programming tomorrow. She doesn't have time to go to the store. She calls Tom at work. John, the receptionist, answers.*

JOHN: Good afternoon, Winfield Travel. May I help you?

ADELA: Tom Logan, please. This is his wife calling.

JOHN: He's on the other line. Can you hold?

ADELA: Sure.

TOM: Hello. Tom Logan speaking.

ADELA: Hi, hon.

TOM: Oh, hi. How's everything?

ADELA: Fine. I'm studying for my test.

TOM: How's it going?

ADELA: OK, but we need some things from the supermarket. Can you stop there on your way home?

TOM: Sure.

ADELA: We need a pound of ground beef, a half gallon of milk, a dozen eggs, and some fresh vegetables for a salad.

TOM: Anything else?

ADELA: No. That's all.

TOM: OK. See you tonight.

ADELA: Bye.

## 1 Presentation

### Identifying countable and noncountable nouns

A

a tomato
3 tomatoes

C

an orange
4 oranges

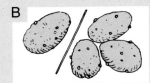
B

a potato
3 potatoes

**Countable nouns**

Countable nouns have singular and plural forms.

D

an apple
2 apples

E

an egg
3 eggs

F
A: What's this?
B: It's a tomato.

G
A: What are these?
B: They're tomatoes.

H

milk

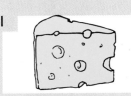
I

cheese

**Noncountable nouns**

Noncountable nouns have a singular form only. They do not use **a** or **an**.

J

meat

K

bread

L

coffee

M
A: What's this?
B: It's milk.

## 2 Practice

Practice with a partner. Ask and answer questions about each picture in *1*. Use conversation models F, G, and M.

## 3 Vocabulary in Context

Shopping in a supermarket

**This is the floor plan of Bell's Supermarket in Winfield.**

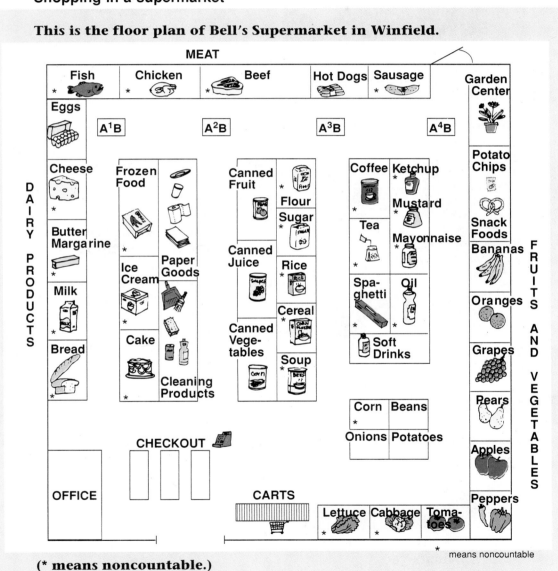

MEAT

| Fish | Chicken | Beef | Hot Dogs | Sausage |

Garden Center

Eggs

A¹B   A²B   A³B   A⁴B

DAIRY PRODUCTS

Cheese
Butter Margarine
Milk
Bread

Frozen Food
Ice Cream
Cake

Paper Goods
Cleaning Products

Canned Fruit
Canned Juice
Canned Vegetables

Flour
Sugar
Rice
Cereal
Soup

Coffee   Ketchup
Tea      Mustard
         Mayonnaise
Spaghetti  Oil
Soft Drinks

Corn   Beans
Onions   Potatoes

Potato Chips
Snack Foods
Bananas
Oranges
Grapes
Pears
Apples
Peppers

FRUITS AND VEGETABLES

CHECKOUT

OFFICE   CARTS

Lettuce   Cabbage   Tomatoes

means noncountable

**(* means noncountable.)**

## 4 Practice

Look at the floor plan of Bell's Supermarket. Take turns pointing to items and identifying them.

> A: What's this?
> B: It's cheese.

> B: What are these?
> A: They're grapes.

## 5 Presentation

**Asking for help in locating food in the supermarket**

| | |
|---|---|
| SHOPPER: | Excuse me, ma'am. Where's the spaghetti? |
| MANAGER: | It's in aisle 3B, **across from** the rice. |
| SHOPPER: | And where are the peppers? |
| MANAGER: | They're **over there, next to** the tomatoes. |
| SHOPPER: | And the margarine? |
| MANAGER: | It's in aisle 1A, **next to** the milk. |
| SHOPPER: | Thank you. |

## 6 Practice

Ask and answer questions about the location of things in Bell's Supermarket (page 69).

> oil / 4A / oranges
> A: Excuse me, | sir. | Where's the oil?
>                  | ma'am. |
> B: It's in aisle 4A, next to the oranges.
> A: Thank you.
> B: You're welcome.

1. flour / 3A / coffee
2. margarine / 1A / milk
3. grapes / over there / oranges
4. cake / 1B / bread
5. hot dogs / over there / sausage
6. sugar / 3A / rice
7. cereal / 3A / soup
8. frozen food / 1B / cheese
9. onions / over there / potatoes
10. soft drinks / over there / corn

**7** Presentation

### Expressing quantity; being general and specific

A

a bottle of ketchup

B

a can of beans

C

a bag of potato chips

D

a loaf of bread

E

five pounds of sugar

F

a quart of milk

G

a dozen eggs

H

a box of cereal

I
a package of hot dogs

J
A: We need some bread.
B: OK. How about two loaves of bread?
A: That's fine. We also need some milk.
B: OK. How about a quart of milk?
A: No. We need a half gallon of milk.

**Irregular plurals:**

1 loaf    →2 loaves
1 dozen →2 dozen

2 pints (pt)  = 1 quart (qt)
2 quarts = 1 half gallon
4 quarts = 1 gallon (gal)

16 ounces (oz) = 1 pound (lb)

## 8 Pronunciation

**Pronounce these phrases.**

some ketchup    a bottle of ketchup    two bottles of ketchup

some rice    a pound of rice    three pounds of rice

some beans    a can of beans    four cans of beans

some bread    a loaf of bread    two loaves of bread

some eggs    a dozen eggs    two dozen eggs

## 9 Practice

**Look at the shopping list.  Work with a partner or in a small group.  Decide how much of each item you want to buy.  Follow the conversation model in** *7.*

```
bread          bananas
milk           apples
eggs           rice
cheese         soup
cereal         oil
tomatoes       ketchup
peppers        sugar
beans          onions
carrots        potato chips
```

## 10 Listening

**Number your paper from 1–10.  Listen to Adela dictate a shopping list.  It includes the same items as the list in** *9.*  **The first time you listen, just write the item. The second time, fill in the quantity.**

| FIRST TIME YOU HEAR: | I need two quarts of milk. |
| WRITE: | _____ milk _____ |
| SECOND TIME: | I need two quarts of milk. |
| WRITE: | _____ two quarts of milk _____ |

## 11 Presentation 🔲

**Asking for a favor**

ADELA: See you later, Elinor. I have to go to the supermarket.
ELINOR: Adela, can you do me a favor?
ADELA: Sure. What?
ELINOR: I need five pounds of sugar and a dozen eggs.
ADELA: Anything else?
ELINOR: No, that's all. Thanks.

## 12 Pronunciation 🔲

**Repeat these phrases.**

1. apples, oranges, grapes, and pears
2. flour, sugar, rice, and cereal
3. lettuce, tomatoes, onions, and corn

**Repeat these sentences.**

4. I need some soup, some onions, and some bananas.
5. We need a pound of apples, three cans of beans, and a bag of potato chips.

## 13 Interaction

**You need two or three items at the supermarket. Ask a classmate for a favor.**

A: See you later, _____ . I have to go to the supermarket.
B: _____ , can you do me a favor?
A: Sure. What?
B: I need _____ and _____ .
A: Anything else?
B: No, that's all. Thanks.

## 14 Reading

### Before You Read

1. Where do you find supermarket advertisements?
2. What items are listed in the ads? Everything in the store?

Bell's Supermarket

**SUMMER FAVORITES ON SALE**

**SUPER DISCOUNT!!**

### Meat

USDA Choice
Boneless Sirloin Steak
$2.69 lb.

USDA GRADE A
10 – 14 lb. AVG.
Fresh Young Turkey
79¢ lb.

### Fruit and Vegetables

California Melons
cantaloupe
88¢ ea.
watermelon
18¢ lb.

LARGE
Slicing tomatoes...88¢ lb.
Fresh peas.............79¢ lb.
Lettuce..................89¢ head
Onions...................39¢ lb.

### After You Read

**Read the statement and say** *That's right, That's wrong,* **or** *I don't know.*

1. Chicken is on sale.
2. Onions are on sale.
3. The tomatoes are small.
4. The lettuce is from California.
5. A cantaloupe is a melon.
6. The cantaloupe is from California.
7. The turkey is frozen.
8. The supermarket is on Ocean Avenue.

## 15 Writing

You are having a party for 25 people. Write a shopping list of things you need. Write a quantity next to each item on the list. Share your list with a classmate.

## 16 Final Activity

You are going to the supermarket. You meet a friend on the street. Make up a conversation following these instructions. Practice it and role play it for the class.

| | |
|---|---|
| A: | Greet B. |
| B: | Respond. Ask where A is going. |
| A: | Say "the supermarket" and ask B to come along. |
| B: | Say you can't. Say you have a dentist appointment. Ask A to do you a favor. |
| A: | Say "yes" and ask what. |
| B: | Name the the items you need. |
| A: | Ask if there is anything else. |
| B: | Say "no" and "thank you." |

COMMUNICATION

Talking about residence, work, and school ▪ Talking about a person's schedule ▪ Asking for and giving an opinion

GRAMMAR

Simple present tense: third person singular; affirmative and negative statements; yes/no questions, and short answers with *does* ▪ *When*: asking about time ▪ Prepositions: *on* + days of the week; *from* + time + *to* + time; day + *through* + day; *at* night, *at* + time ▪ Adjective + noun

# TV Recipe

*It's Saturday afternoon. Gloria is at Bob's house.*

GLORIA: What time is it, Bob?
BOB: It's noon. Why?
GLORIA: "TV Recipe" is on at noon. Would you please turn on the TV? I want to write down today's recipe .
BOB: Sure. What channel?
GLORIA: Six, I think.

ANNOUNCER: Good afternoon, everyone. I'm Jack Anderson. Welcome to "TV Recipe." Our cook today is my good friend, Gino Leone. Gino lives in Winfield, but he comes from Italy originally. He works at the Roma Restaurant on Prince Street. He also teaches cooking every Saturday morning at the community college. Gino is a great cook and an excellent teacher. He makes a terrific spaghetti sauce. After a word from our sponsor, we'll make the Roma Sauce with Gino.

GLORIA: Oh, no! Not another commercial!

ANNOUNCER: Here we are at the home of Paul and Kate Johnson. Let's go into the kitchen. Hello, Kate. Hello, Paul. Are you busy today?

PAUL: Yes, we are. We're cleaning the kitchen.

ANNOUNCER: And what are you using?

KATE: We're using MARV.

ANNOUNCER: Does MARV clean well?

PAUL: It sure does. MARV is marvelous. Just look at this marvelous kitchen!

ANNOUNCER: Kate and Paul Johnson are smart. They're using MARV. MARV is marvelous.

GLORIA: What a dumb commercial!

BOB: Yeah. It's really awful!

## 1 Presentation

### Talking about residence, work, and school

| Use the simple present tense to talk about a person's daily life. | He lives<br>She works  in Winfield.<br>He teaches |
|---|---|

1. Gino Leone **lives** in Winfield, New York.
2. He **works** at the Roma Restaurant.
3. He **makes** the Roma Sauce every day.
4. He **teaches** cooking at the community college.
5. Sam Logan **lives** in Winfield.
6. He **works** at the Winfield Garage.
7. He **fixes** cars during the day.
8. He **goes** to the community college at night.
9. He **studies** engineering.
10. Adela Logan **works** at home.
11. She **takes care of** her home and family.
12. She **studies** computer programming at the Technical Institute.

**Irregular:**
go: | he<br>she | goes
have: | he<br>she | has

## 2 Pronunciation

**Pronounce each column of verbs.**

| **1.** /z/ | **2.** /s/ | **3.** /ɪz/ |
|---|---|---|
| lives | works | teaches |
| goes | makes | fixes |
| has | takes care of | washes |
| studies | speaks | watches |
| drives | cooks | relaxes |
| listens | | dances |
| cleans | | |
| calls | | |
| plays | | |
| reads | | |
| swims | | |

## 3 Practice

**Make sentences about the *Intercom 2000* characters.**

> Mike / student // go / Winfield H.S.
>
> Mike is a student.  He goes to Winfield High School.

1. Tom / travel agent // live / Winfield
2. Elinor / doctor // work / Winfield Hospital
3. Bob / student // go / Winfield H.S.
4. Sam / mechanic // fix / cars
5. Gino / cook // make / the Roma Sauce every day
6. Liz / telephone operator // live / Winfield
7. Adela / homemaker // take care of / her family
8. Adela / student // study / computer programming
9. Gino / cook // teach / cooking
10. Cristina / restaurant cashier // live and work / Winfield

## 4 Presentation 🔲

### Talking about a person's schedule

| | | Days | Hours |
|---|---|---|---|
| **Gino** | (work) | Tuesday-Saturday | 3:00 PM -11:00 PM |
| | (teach) | Saturday | 8:00 AM -12:00 noon |
| **Cristina** | (work) | Tuesday-Saturday | 11:00 AM - 7:00 PM |
| **Sam** | (work) | Monday-Friday | 8:00 AM - 5:00 PM |
| | (class) | Tuesday and Thursday | 7:00 PM -10:00 PM |
| **Adela** | (class) | Monday-Friday | 8:00 AM -12:00 noon |

1. Gino works **on** Tuesday, Wednesday, Thursday, Friday, and Saturday.
2. He works Tuesday **through** Saturday.
3. He works **from** 3:00 **to** 11:00.
4. He teaches cooking **on** Saturday morning.
5. He teaches **from** 8:00 **to** 12:00.
6. Adela has class Monday **through** Friday.
7. She has class **from** 8:00 **to** 12:00.
8. Sam has class **at night** from 7:00 to 10:00.

## 5 Practice

**Look at the schedule in 4. Make statements about the characters.**

1. Gino / work / . . .through . . .
2. Cristina / work / from . . .to
3. Adela / have class / . . .through . . .
4. Adela / have class / from . . .to
5. Gino / work / from . . .to
6. Sam / have class / on
7. Cristina / work / . . .through . . .
8. Sam / work / from . . .to
9. Gino / teach / on
10. Gino / teach / from . . .to

## 6 Practice

Complete these sentences about yourself, then tell your classmates about your schedule.

1. | I work at _____ .
   | I go to _____ .

2. I | work
     | have class | _____ through _____ .

   I | work
     | have class | on _____ , _____ , and _____ .

3. I | work
     | have class | from _____ to _____ .

## 7 Presentation 🔊

**Asking about a person's schedule**

| Does | he<br>she | work on Monday? | | Yes, | he<br>she | does. | | No, | he<br>she | doesn't. |
|------|-----------|-----------------|---|------|-----------|-------|---|-----|-----------|----------|

A
> A: Does Gino work at the Roma?
> B: Yes, he does.

B
> A: Does he work on Monday?
> B: No, he doesn't.

C
> A: Does Adela study computer programming?
> B: Yes, she does.

D
> A: Does she have class at night?
> B: No, she doesn't.

## 8 Practice

Look at the schedule in 4, page 79. With a partner, ask and answer questions about people's schedules. Use the conversation models in 7.

1. Cristina / work / Monday
2. Gino / work / at night
3. Sam / work / from 9:00-5:00

4. Adela / have class / Monday through Friday
5. Cristina / teach / cooking
6. Gino / work / Saturday
7. Sam / work / Tuesday through Saturday
8. Adela / have class / at night
9. Cristina / work / Sunday
10. Gino / teach / Wednesday

## 9 Interaction

**Write the names of five friends or family members who work on a piece of paper.
Exchange lists with a partner. For each person, find out if he/she works . . .**

1. . . . Monday through Friday
2. . . . on Saturday
3. . . . from 9:00-5:00
4. . . . at night

> A: Does _____ work Monday through Friday?
> B: | Yes, _____ .
>    | No, _____ . \_\_\_\_\_ works _____ .

## 10 Presentation

### Finding out when a person can do something

| Their Days Off | | |
| --- | --- | --- |
| **Gino** | Sunday | Monday |
| **Cristina** | Sunday | Monday |
| **Bob** | Saturday | Sunday |
| **Gloria** | Saturday | Sunday |

A **day off** is a day you don't work or go to school.

A
> A: Can Bob go to New York on Saturday?
> B: Yes, he can. He doesn't have class on Saturday.

B
> A: Can Cristina go to New York on Saturday?
> B: No, she can't. She works on Saturday.

## 11 Practice

Work with a partner. Look at the chart in *10*. Ask if the people can go to New York on Saturday, Sunday, and Monday.

## 12 Listening 📟

Number your paper from 1-10. Look at the schedule in *4*, page 79. Listen and write the person's name.

| | |
|---|---|
| YOU HEAR: | She doesn't have class on Saturday. |
| WRITE: | _____Adela_____ |

## 13 Writing

Write a paragraph about a friend or family member. Write about what he/she does and his/her schedule. Use this paragraph as a model.

> *My Brother's Schedule*
>
> *Pablo Soto is my brother. He is a librarian. He works at the library on First Street. He works Monday through Friday from 8:30 to 4:30. He works on Saturday morning from 8:30 to 12:00. He doesn't work on Saturday afternoon or on Sunday.*

## 14 Presentation

**Asking for and giving an opinion**

> BOB: Do you like "TV Recipe?"
> GLORIA: Yes, it's an interesting program. Do you like the MARV commercial?
> BOB: No, it's an awful commercial.

## 15 Practice

Give an opinion using the cues and one of these adjectives: *good, great, terrific, excellent, awful, dumb, marvelous, interesting, or beautiful.* Follow the conversation model in *14.*

1. TV Recipe / program
2. the Roma / restaurant
3. Winfield / town
4. the MARV commercial / commercial
5. Winfield Park / park

6. the Chinese restaurant / restaurant
7. Bell's / supermarket
8. the Roma Sauce / sauce
9. New York / city
10. *Intercom 2000* / book

## 16 Interaction

List TV programs, commercials, restaurants, stores, or cities and towns that you know. Share your opinions of them.

| A: Do you like _____ ? |
| B: | Yes, | _____ . |
|    | No,  | |

## 17 Presentation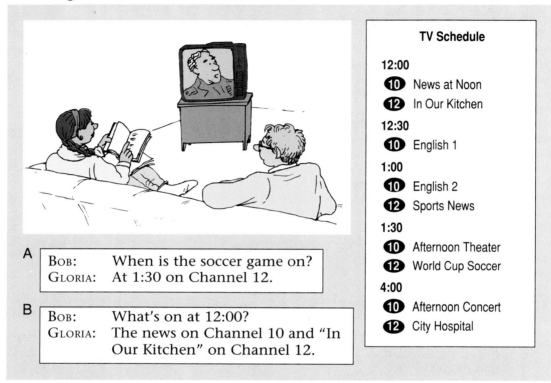

### Talking about time and TV schedules

**TV Schedule**

**12:00**
- ⑩ News at Noon
- ⑫ In Our Kitchen

**12:30**
- ⑩ English 1

**1:00**
- ⑩ English 2
- ⑫ Sports News

**1:30**
- ⑩ Afternoon Theater
- ⑫ World Cup Soccer

**4:00**
- ⑩ Afternoon Concert
- ⑫ City Hospital

**A**

BOB: When is the soccer game on?
GLORIA: At 1:30 on Channel 12.

**B**

BOB: What's on at 12:00?
GLORIA: The news on Channel 10 and "In Our Kitchen" on Channel 12.

## 18 Practice

**Work with a partner. Look at the TV schedule. Ask about the different programs. Follow the conversation models in *17*.**

## 19 Interaction

**Suggest a program from the TV schedule in *17*. Your partner disagrees and gives an opinion.**

A: Let's watch _____ .
B: No, it's a _____ program. Let's watch _____ .
A: OK. When is it on?
B: At _____ on Channel ____ .

# Reading

## Before You Read

1. Do you use a TV guide?
2. What information can you find in a TV guide?

## After You Read

**Check the TV guide and answer the questions.**

1. What's on Channel 6 at 7:30?
2. What's on Channel 6 from 8:30-9:30?
3. What time is the movie on? What channel?
4. What are the names of two sports programs?
5. What are the names of two music programs?

| | Monday afternoon and evening | |
|---|---|---|
| 4:00 | **6** | Children's Hour |
| | **7** | Cartoons |
| 4:30 | **6** | Cartoons |
| | **7** | Disney Hour |
| 5:00 | **6** | Evening News |
| 5:30 | **7** | It's Your Business |
| 6:00 | **6** | This Old House |
| | **7** | Evening News |
| 7:00 | **6** | Week in Rock |
| | **7** | It's a Small World |
| 7:30 | **6** | My Five Sons |
| | **7** | Sports World |
| 8:00 | **6** | Family Doctor |
| | **7** | Monday Night Baseball |
| 8:30 | **6** | Big City Police |
| 9:30 | **6** | The Z-Team |
| 10:30 | **6** | Cinema 6: Who's That Girl? |
| 11:00 | **7** | Late News |
| 11:30 | **7** | Late Night Concert |
| 12:00 | **6** | Late Late News |

## 21 Final Activity

This is Cindy. She doesn't like to relax. She likes to be busy all the time. With a partner, write a list of all the things that Cindy does on a typical day. Also write when she does each activity. Use these pictures, and three ideas of your own.

COMMUNICATION
Giving instructions ▪ Commenting on food ▪
Asking about quantity and number

GRAMMAR
Imperatives ▪ *Look, smell, taste* + adjective ▪
Simple present tense: Wh-questions with
*What, How much,* and *How many* ▪
Prepositions: *for* + time; *with*

# The Roma Sauce

GINO: Good afternoon, everyone. I'm Gino Leone. I come from Italy, and I like to cook Italian food. My favorite dish is spaghetti with mushroom sauce. My favorite sauce is the Roma Sauce. Let's make it together.

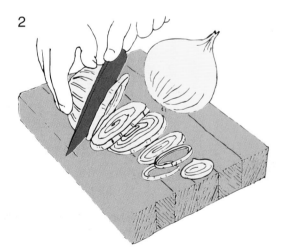

First, pour three tablespoons of oil into a large frying pan.

1

Next, slice two onions. Put the onions and some garlic in the oil. Cook the onions and garlic for three minutes.

2

3

Now add one pound of sliced mushrooms. Cook the mushrooms, onion, and garlic for ten minutes.

Next, add one small can of tomato paste, one large can of tomatoes, and two cups of water.

4

5

Finally, season the sauce with salt, pepper, oregano, and basil. Mmmm. It smells delicious. Now cook the sauce for one hour over low heat, and you have the Roma Sauce. Serve the sauce on spaghetti with Parmesan cheese.

ANNOUNCER: Thank you, Gino. Ladies and gentlemen, don't go away. I'll be right back to tell you how to get a copy of the recipe for the Roma Sauce.

**1** **Presentation** 🔲

### Giving instructions

> Use the imperative form to give instructions.
> The imperative form is the same as the base form of a verb.

1. **Pour** three tablespoons of oil into a large pan.
2. **Slice** two onions.
3. **Put** the onions in the oil.
4. **Cook** the onions for three minutes.
5. **Add** one pound of sliced mushrooms.
6. **Season** the sauce.

**2** **Practice**

**Practice with a partner. Give him/her instructions for making the Roma Sauce. Use the pictures on pages 86-87 as cues.**

**Presentation** 🔲

**Prepositions *for* and *with***

1. Cook the onions **for** three minutes.
2. Cook the sauce **for** one hour.
3. My favorite dish is spaghetti **with** mushroom sauce.
4. Season the sauce **with** salt, pepper, oregano, and basil.
5. We can make the Roma Sauce **with** Gino.


**4** **Practice**

**Read each sentence aloud with the correct preposition. Use *for* or *with*.**

1. Gino cooks the Roma Sauce _____ an hour.
2. He seasons the sauce _____ oregano.
3. Bob plays tennis _____ Gloria and Mike.
4. They play _____ two hours on Saturday.
5. Joyce goes to the pool _____ Lisa.
6. They swim _____ an hour or two.
7. Gino relaxes _____ two hours after the class at the community college.
8. On Sunday he goes to a movie _____ Cristina.
9. Adela studies _____ two hours every evening.
10. Then she relaxes _____ Tom.


**5** **Reentry**

**Prepositions**

**Complete each sentence with the correct preposition. Use: *in, on, at, to, of, for, with.***

1. Gino Leone teaches cooking _____ the community college _____ College Avenue _____ Winfield, New York.
2. He goes _____ the community college every Saturday morning.
3. He makes the Roma Sauce _____ every new class.
4. He pours three tablespoons _____ oil into a large frying pan.
5. He slices two onions. He puts the onions _____ the pan.

6. He cooks the onions _____ three minutes.
7. He adds one pound _____ sliced mushrooms.
8. He cooks the mushrooms and onions _____ ten minutes.
9. He adds tomato paste, tomatoes, and two cups _____ water.
10. He seasons the sauce _____ salt, pepper, oregano, and basil.
11. He cooks the sauce _____ one hour.
12. He serves the Roma Sauce on spaghetti _____ Parmesan cheese.

## 6 Presentation

### Giving instructions

## 7 Pronunciation

**Repeat the instructions.**

1. Use margarine. Don't use butter.

2. Buy sausage. Don't buy hot dogs.

3. Buy fresh tomatoes. Don't buy canned tomatoes.

4. Use fresh juice. Don't use frozen juice.

5. Use a small onion. Don't use a large onion.

**Useful vocabulary:**

canned = in a can

## 8 Practice

Work with a partner. Take turns giving instructions from the cues. Use *buy* or *use*.
Follow the conversation model in *6*.

1. hot dogs / not sausage
2. cabbage / not lettuce
3. butter / not margarine
4. milk / not water

5. fresh juice / not frozen juice
6. fresh beans / not canned beans
7. fresh corn / not frozen corn
8. dry bread / not fresh bread

## 9 Presentation

**Commenting on how food looks, smells, and tastes**

A

  Look at this cake.   It looks good.

  Smell this cake.    It smells good, too.

Taste this cake.    It tastes delicious.

B

Look at these apples.   They look nice and fresh.

Smell these apples.   They smell fresh, too.

Taste these apples.   They taste great.

C

Look at this bread.   It looks old and dry.

Taste it.    It tastes awful.

## 10 Practice

**Tell a classmate to *look at*, *smell*, or *taste* something, depending on the symbol.**

ice cream / delicious
A: Look at this ice cream.
B: It looks delicious!

onions / awful
A: Smell these onions.
B: They smell awful!

1. fresh bread / terrific
2. spaghetti sauce / great
3. grapes / delicious
4. apple / very good
5. old onions / awful

6. soup / OK
7. pears / delicious
8. lettuce / nice and fresh
9. coffee / awful
10. ice cream / good

## 11 Interaction

**Ask your partner to look at, smell, or taste something.**

| A: | _____ | this these | _____ . |
|---|---|---|---|
| B: | It They | _____ . | |

## 12 Listening

**Number your paper from 1-4. Listen to the conversations and write what the cook is making.**

| YOU HEAR: | ADELA: | Let's see. I have chicken, carrots, onions, peppers, garlic, and water. |
|---|---|---|
| | BOB: | What are you making, Mom? |
| WRITE: | | _____soup_____ |
| YOU HEAR: | ADELA: | Soup, Bob. |

## 13 Presentation

### Asking about quantity and number

| Wh-questions: simple present tense | |
|---|---|
| What<br>How many tomatoes<br>How much oil | does Bob need? |

Bob is cooking for Adela and Tom. He is making spaghetti with the Roma Sauce and a salad. Here is his shopping list.

Use **how many** with plural countable nouns.
Use **how much** with noncountable nouns.

1 small bottle of oil
2 large onions
1 pound of fresh mushrooms
1 small can of tomato paste
1 large can of tomatoes
1 pound of spaghetti
½ pound of parmesan cheese
1 head of lettuce
2 fresh tomatoes
1 large pepper

**A**
A: What does Bob need?
B: He needs some lettuce.
A: How much does he need?
B: One head.

**B**
A: What does Bob need?
B: He needs some fresh tomatoes.
A: How many does he need?
B: Two.

## 14 Practice

Work with a partner. Look at Bob's shopping list. Ask and answer questions using *what*, *how much*, or *how many*.

## 15 Interaction

You're cooking today. Write the recipe for your favorite dish and talk to your partner about it.

A: I'm making _____ . I need some _____ .
B: How _____ do you need?
A: _____ . I need some _____ too.
B: How _____ do you need?
A: _____ .

## 16 Reading

### Before You Read

**1.** What information is in a recipe?
**2.** What are common measurements in a recipe?

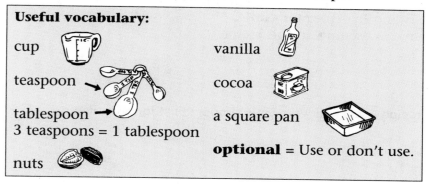

**Useful vocabulary:**

cup

teaspoon ➔

tablespoon ➔
3 teaspoons = 1 tablespoon

nuts

vanilla

cocoa

a square pan

**optional** = Use or don't use.

*Many Americans like to eat brownies. Brownies are a kind of cake. This is the recipe.*

```
BROWNIES

1/2 cup flour                    2 eggs
1 cup sugar                      1 teaspoon vanilla
2 tablespoons cocoa powder       1/2 cup chopped nuts
a pinch of salt                        (optional)
1/2 cup melted butter
     or margarine


Combine the dry ingredients.  Mix well.
Combine butter, eggs, and vanilla, and add to dry
ingredients.  Mix well. (Add the chopped nuts.) Pour
into greased square pan and bake at 350° for 30
minutes.  Cool and cut into squares.
Serve with vanilla ice cream.  Serves 8.
```

*After You Read*

**Read each sentence. Say** *That's right*, *That's wrong*, **or** *I don't know.*

1. A teaspoon is a small spoon.
2. First you combine and mix the flour, sugar, salt, and butter.
3. You cook the brownies for 350 minutes.
4. **Bake** is another word for **cook.**
5. You have to use nuts in this recipe.

## 17 Writing

Check the recipe again and write your shopping list for brownies.

## 18 Final Activity

Talk with your classmates about your favorite foods for breakfast, lunch, or dinner. Answer the questions below.

> **Useful vocabulary:**
>
> **breakfast** = the meal you eat in the morning
>
> **lunch** = the meal you eat at noon
>
> **dinner** = the meal you eat in the evening

1. What do you eat for breakfast?
2. Does your country have a special breakfast dish or food?
   What is the name of the dish or food?
   What ingredients do you need?
   How do you make it?
3. Does your country have a special lunch or dinner dish?
   What is the name of the dish?
   What ingredients do you need?
   How do you make it?

COMMUNICATION
Describing how you feel ▪ Making and accepting suggestions ▪ Discussing what you want to eat ▪ Ordering in a restaurant ▪ Talking about prices

GRAMMAR
*Be* + hungry, thirsty ▪ *What kind of* + noun ▪ *Want* + noun ▪ *Would like* + noun ▪ *How much*

# At the Roma

*It's Saturday afternoon. Bob and Sam Logan are at the college library. Sam is helping Bob with his math.*

BOB:   Boy, I'm tired and hungry.

SAM:   Me too. Why don't we get some pizza at the Roma?

BOB:   Good idea ... but how much is a pizza there?

SAM:   Not much. About $7.00. We can split it.

BOB:   I only have $2.50. Can I borrow a couple of bucks?

SAM:   Sure, but you're always broke. You need a part-time job.

BOB:   I know. I'm thinking about getting one.

SAM:   What kind of pizza do you want, Bob?

BOB:   How about a large combination?

SAM:   Sounds good to me. What do you want to drink?

BOB:   A cola.

WAITER:   Would you like to order now?

SAM:   Yes. We'd like a large combination pizza and two large colas.

WAITER:   Would you like anything else? A salad maybe?

SAM:   No, thanks.

WAITER:   OK. One large combination pizza and two large colas.

## 1 Presentation

### Describing how you feel; making and accepting suggestions

A

| | |
|---|---|
| LIZ: | Boy, I'm hungry. |
| ELINOR: | Me too. Let's get something to eat. |
| LIZ: | Good idea. Why don't we go to the Chinese restaurant? |
| ELINOR: | Fine with me. |

B

| | |
|---|---|
| BOB: | I'm thirsty. |
| MIKE: | Me too. Let's get something to drink. |
| BOB: | Sounds good to me. Why don't we go to the Roma? |
| MIKE: | OK with me. |

## 2 Interaction

**Make a list of several restaurants in your city. Then work with a partner.
Complete this conversation and role play it for the class.**

A: Boy, I'm _____ !
B: Me too. Let's _____ .
A: _____ . Why don't we go _____ ?
B: _____ .

**Discussing what you want to eat**

| | By the Slice | Small | Medium | Large |
|---|---|---|---|---|
| PIZZAS • PIZZAS • PIZZAS • PIZZAS | | | | |
| cheese (plain) | .75 | 4.25 | 5.50 | 6.75 |
| sausage | 1.00 | 4.75 | 6.00 | 7.25 |
| pepperoni | 1.00 | 4.75 | 6.00 | 7.25 |
| mushroom & sausage | 1.50 | 5.25 | 6.50 | 7.75 |
| pepper & onion | 1.50 | 5.25 | 6.50 | 7.75 |
| combination | 2.00 | 6.25 | 7.50 | 9.00 |

1. A **plain pizza** has only cheese on it.
2. A pizza with sausage on it is a **sausage pizza.**
3. A pizza with mushrooms and sausage is a **mushroom and sausage pizza.**
4. A pizza with everything on it is a **combination pizza.**

A

a slice of pizza

B

a glass of water

C

a cola
a glass of cola

D

an orange soda
a glass of orange soda

E

| | |
|---|---|
| SAM: | What kind of pizza do you want, Bob? |
| BOB: | How about a large combination? |
| SAM: | OK. What do you want to drink? |
| BOB: | A cola. |

## 4 Practice

**Work with a partner. Discuss what kind of pizza you want and what you want to drink. Follow the conversation model in 3.**

1. medium mushroom and sausage / a glass of water
2. small pepperoni / a glass of cola
3. large cheese and mushroom / an orange soda
4. large pepper and onion / a glass of water
5. plain pizza / a glass of cola

## 5 Presentation

**Ordering food in a restaurant; saying what you want politely**

a waiter

a waitress

| | |
|---|---|
| WAITER: | Good afternoon. Would you like to order now? |
| HOWARD: | Yes. I'd like a slice of plain pizza. |
| WAITER: | And you, ma'am? |
| ELINOR: | I'd like a slice of sausage pizza. |
| WAITER: | And you, sir? |
| TED: | I'd like spaghetti, please. |
| WAITER: | Would you like something to drink? |
| ELINOR: | A glass of water, please. |
| TED: | Orange soda for me. |
| HOWARD: | A cup of coffee, please. |
| WAITER: | Anything else? |
| HOWARD: | No, thanks. That's all. |

## 6 Pronunciation 📼

**Repeat these sentences.**

1. Would you like to order now?
   /wʊjə/

2. I'd like a pizza.
   /aɪ dlaɪk/

3. I'd like a slice of pizza.

4. I'd like a slice of sausage pizza.

5. We'd like a pizza.
   /wi dlaɪk/

6. We'd like a sausage pizza.

7. We'd like a large sausage pizza.

## 7 Practice

**Work with a partner. Take turns being the waiter or waitress. Order for yourself or for you and your friends.**

slice / plain

A: Would you like to order now?
B: Yes. I'd like a slice of plain pizza.

large / pepperoni

A: Would you like to order now?
B: Yes. We'd like a large pepperoni pizza.

1. slice / sausage
2. large / pepper and onion
3. medium / plain
4. small / combination
5. small / sausage
6. medium / combination
7. slice / pepperoni
8. slice / pepper and onion
9. medium / sausage
10. large / mushroom and sausage

## 8 Interaction

Form groups of three students. One student is the waiter or waitress. The other two are the customers. Practice ordering pizza and something to drink.

| | |
|---|---|
| WAITER:<br>WAITRESS: | Good _____ . Would you like to order now? |
| CUSTOMER 1: | Yes. I'd like a _____ . |
| WAITER: | And you, _____ ? |
| CUSTOMER 2: | I'd like a _____ . |
| WAITER: | Would you like something to drink? |
| CUSTOMER 1: | _____ . |
| CUSTOMER 2: | _____ . |
| WAITER: | Anything else? |
| CUSTOMER 1: | _____ . |

## 9 Vocabulary in Context

### Talking about prices

| a penny<br>1 cent | a nickel<br>5 cents | a dime<br>10 cents | a quarter<br>25 cents | a dollar<br>100 cents |
|---|---|---|---|---|

**Price**

| $.65<br>65¢ | sixty-five cents |
|---|---|
| $1.00 | a dollar<br>one dollar |
| $1.05 | a dollar five<br>one dollar and five cents |
| $2.25 | two twenty-five<br>two dollars and twenty-five cents |

A

| BOB: | How much does a small plain pizza cost? |
|---|---|
| SAM: | It costs $4.25. |

B

| BOB: | How much is a medium pepperoni? |
|---|---|
| SAM: | $6.00. |

## 10 Practice

Say the prices.  Then take turns saying the prices to a classmate while he/she writes them.

1. $5.25
2. $6.75
3. $2.98
4. $3.95
5. $1.10

6.  $  4.49
7.  $ 10.50
8.  $  7.99
9.  $  9.00
10.  $  3.45

## 11 Practice

Practice with a partner.  Ask and answer questions about the prices of pizzas in the sign on page 97.  Follow conversation models A and B in *9*.

## 12 Reading

### Before You Read

1. What do you think Americans like to eat for lunch?
2. What's in a typical sandwich?
3. What's in a typical salad?

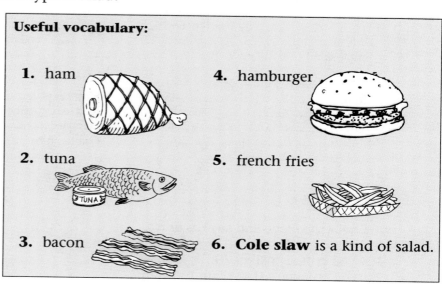

Useful vocabulary:

1. ham
2. tuna
3. bacon
4. hamburger
5. french fries
6. **Cole slaw** is a kind of salad.

# Maggie's

*The best salads, sandwiches, and burgers in town!*

157 Ocean Avenue
Winfield, NY

## MENU

### SALAD PLATES
1. Combination salad - 2 sliced eggs, turkey, lettuce and tomato, cole slaw .....3.75
2. Chicken salad, potato salad, cole slaw, lettuce and tomato ...........................3.50
3. Tuna salad, potato salad, cole slaw, lettuce and tomato ................................3.50

### SANDWICHES
1. Ham and swiss cheese - with cole slaw ..........................................................3.95
2. Corned beef and pastrami - with cole slaw ....................................................4.50
3. Turkey, bacon, and swiss cheese - with cole slaw .........................................4.50

### JUMBO HAMBURGER - *100% PURE BEEF*
On toasted bun with onions and pickles.............................................................1.95
...........................plus lettuce and tomato ......................................................2.25
...........................plus lettuce, tomato, and large  french fries.........................2.95

### CHEESEBURGER  - Jumbo Burger with Melted Cheese
On toasted bun with onions and pickles.............................................................2.25
...........................plus lettuce and tomato ......................................................2.55
...........................plus lettuce, tomato, and large french fries.........................3.25

### SIDE ORDERS
French fries ....................large ...................................................................85
.................................small ...................................................................55
Baked potato.................plain ..................................................................1.50
.................................with cheese .........................................................1.75
.................................with bacon ..........................................................2.25
Cole slaw...........................................................................................................75
Small salad.........................................................................................................95

### BEVERAGES
| | | | |
|---|---|---|---|
| Coffee | .45 | Hot chocolate | .50 |
| Sanka | .50 | Iced tea or coffee | .70 |
| Tea | .40 | Lemonade | .70 |
| Milk | .60 | Orange juice | .85 |

## After You Read

**A.  Check the menu and say *Yes* or *No*.**

1. Iced coffee costs $.70.
2. The chicken salad plate has ham.

**3.** You have $3.00.  Can you get a hamburger, some french fries, and a glass of orange juice?

**4.** You have $2.00.  Can you get a salad plate?

**5.** You are thirsty.  You have $.50.  Can you get a beverage?

**6.** You have $4.00.  Can you get a cheeseburger with lettuce, tomato, and french fries?

### B. Find foods you like.

**1.** If you don't eat meat or fish, what would you order?

**2.** If you like fish or seafood, what would you order?

**3.** If you like meat, what would you order?

## 13 Listening

**Number your paper from 1-10.**

**A (1-5):  Listen to the sentence.  Check the menu and write *yes* or *no*.**

| You hear: | A jumbo hamburger costs $1.95. |
|---|---|
| Write: | Yes |

**B (6-10):  Listen to the conversation, check the menu, and write the price of what the person orders.**

| You hear: | Would you like to order now?<br>Yes.  A side order of cole slaw, please. |
|---|---|
| Write: | $.75 |

## 14 Final Activity

Work in groups of three.  Make a simple menu that includes prices.  Then, write a conversation following the instructions below.  Role play the conversation for the class.

| Waiter:<br>Waitress: | Greet the customers.  Ask if they would like to order. |
|---|---|
| Customers: | Give your lunch orders. |
| Waiter: | Ask the customers if they want anything else. |
| Customer 1: | Respond politely. |
| Waiter: | Repeat the orders. |

COMMUNICATION
Talking about routine activities ▪
Asking about when people do things ▪
Talking about age

GRAMMAR
Simple present tense: Affirmative and
negative statements; Yes/no questions and
short answers with *do*; Wh-question:
*when* ▪ Prepositions: *in* + the morning/
afternoon/evening; *during* the week;
*on* + the weekend/weekends

# A Busy Family

*The Logans are a busy family. Tom Logan works at Wells Travel Agency. Adela
Logan manages the home and studies computer programming.*

*The Logans have three children. Lisa is 12 and is in the sixth grade at
Winfield Elementary School. Bob is 17 and goes to Winfield High. Sam is 20.
During the day, he works as a mechanic at Winfield Garage. At night, he studies
engineering at Winfield Community College.*

*On the weekend, the Logans have a lot of work around the house. They
also like to relax and have a little fun.*

*It's Saturday morning.*

LISA: Bye, Mom. I'm going to
the park.
ADELA: Wait a minute, Lisa. This is
your week to do the laundry.
LISA: No, it isn't. It's Bob's week.
This is my week to clean the
bathrooms, and I'm finished.

ADELA: Bob, this is your week to do
the laundry.
BOB: Can I do it this afternoon? I have a
lot of homework. I want to study
this morning.
ADELA: C'mon Bob. You can do the laundry
and study at the same time.
BOB: Oh, OK.

## 1 Presentation 🔊

### Talking about routine activities

**Affirmative**

| I<br>You<br>We<br>They | study | during<br>the week. |
|---|---|---|
| He<br>She | studies | |

**Negative**

| I<br>You<br>We<br>They | don't have class | on the<br>weekend. |
|---|---|---|
| He<br>She | doesn't have class | |

A

I **work** at Wells Travel Agency. I **don't work** in the yard during the week. I **work** in the yard on the weekend.

> Use the simple present tense to talk about daily or routine activities.

B

During the week, I **study** computer programming. I **don't have** class on Saturday. On the weekend, I **cook** and **study**.

C

I **work** at Winfield Garage during the week. I **don't work** on Saturday. On the weekend, I **take care of** the family cars.

D

We **don't clean** the apartment during the week. We **don't have** time. On Saturday, we **share** the housework and the yard work.

E

During the week, the children **wash** the dishes. They **help** in the kitchen, and they **study.** They **don't do the laundry,** and they **don't wash** the cars or the dog.

**Practice**

Complete the sentences about the Logans.  Use the affirmative or the negative of
the verb in parentheses ( ).

  **1.** The Logans  _____ (clean) the apartment during the week.
  **2.** Adela  _____ (have) class during the week.
  **3.** Tom  _____ (work) in the yard during the week.
  **4.** The Logans  _____ (share) the housework on the weekend.
  **5.** The children  _____ (wash) the cars during the week.
  **6.** Adela  _____ (cook) and  _____ (study) on
      the weekend.
  **7.** Bob and Lisa  _____ (wash) the dishes during the week.
  **8.** Lisa and Bob  _____ (clean) the apartment during the week.
  **9.** Sam  _____ (take care of) the family cars during the week.
**10.** Tom  _____ (work) in the yard on the weekend.

## 3

**Practice**

| Name | During the Week | On Saturday/On the Weekend |
|---|---|---|
| **Adela** | has class<br>studies | cooks<br>studies |
| **Tom** | goes to work<br>washes the dishes | cooks<br>works in the yard |
| **Sam** | goes to work<br>has class at night | takes care of the family cars<br>works in the yard |
| **Bob** | goes to school<br>studies<br>washes the dishes | cleans the apartment<br>studies<br>does the laundry |
| **Lisa** | goes to school<br>helps in the kitchen | cleans the apartment<br>does the laundry |

Look at the chart.  Write ten sentences about what the Logans *do* and *don't do*
during the week and on the weekend.

> The Logans don't clean the apartment during the week.  They clean
> the apartment on the weekend.
>
> Bob washes the dishes during the week.  He doesn't do the laundry
> during the week.

## 4 Presentation

### Asking about a person's routine activities

| Do | I you we they | study on the weekend? | Yes, | I you we they | do. | No, | I you we they | don't. |
|----|---------------|------------------------|------|----------------|-----|-----|----------------|--------|
| Does | he she | | Yes, | he she | does. | No, | he she | doesn't. |

**A**
A: Do the Logans share the housework?
B: Yes, they do.

**D**
A: Does she clean the apartment during the week?
B: No, she doesn't.

**B**
A: Do they clean the apartment during the week?
B: No, they don't.

**E**
A: Do you have class during the week?
B: Yes, I do.

**C**
A: Does Adela study during the week?
B: Yes, she does.

**F**
A: Do you have class on Saturday?
B: No, I don't.

## 5 Practice

**Look at the chart in 3. With a partner, ask and answer questions about the Logans' activities during the week and on the weekend.**

1. Logans / share the housework / weekend
2. Logans / clean the apartment / week
3. Sam / take care of the family cars / Saturday
4. Bob and Lisa / do the laundry / week
5. Lisa / clean the apartment / week
6. Adela and Tom / cook / weekend
7. Sam / go to work / week
8. Bob / study / weekend
9. Tom / work in the yard / week
10. the children / go to school / weekend

## 6  Interaction

**Work with a partner. Find out if your partner does these things.**

1. Do you study on the weekend?
2. Do you cook during the week?
3. Do you clean the house during the week?
4. Do you do the laundry during the week?
5. Do you go to the supermarket on the weekend?
6. Do you watch TV on the weekend?
7. Do you listen to music during the week?
8. Do you read a newspaper during the week?
9. Do you run or jog during the week?
10. Do you play volleyball or basketball on the weekend?

## 7  Presentation

### Asking about when people do things

| A Typical Saturday | | | |
|---|---|---|---|
| | **Morning** | **Afternoon** | **Evening** |
| **Adela** | cooks and cleans | studies | reads; listens to music |
| **Tom** | cooks | works in the yard | reads; watches TV |
| **Sam** | takes care of the family cars | studies | goes out with friends |
| **Bob** | cleans the apartment; does the laundry | studies | goes out with friends |
| **Lisa** | cleans the apartment | plays with friends | reads or studies; watches a little TV |

A

A: When does Adela cook?
B: She cooks in the morning.

B

A: When do Bob and Sam study?
B: They study in the afternoon.

**C**
A: When does Sam take care of the family cars?
B: | On Saturday morning. |
  | Saturday morning. |

**D**
A: When do the Logans relax?
B: | On Saturday evening. |
  | Saturday evening. |

**E**
A: Do you go out on Saturday?
B: Yes, I do.
A: When do you go out?
B: In the evening.

## 8 Pronunciation

**Pronounce these questions.**

1. Does Adela cook?

2. When does she cook?

3. Do the children do the laundry?

4. When do they do the laundry?

5. Do you go out?

6. When do you go out?

## 9 Practice

Work with a partner. Look at the chart in 7. Ask and answer questions about each of the Logans' Saturday activities. Also ask about: Adela and Tom; Bob and Sam; and Bob and Lisa.

## 10 Interaction

Work with a group of four or five. Find out how many people in your group do these things. Find out when. One person reports to the class.

1. Do you read a newspaper?
2. When do you read the newspaper?
3. Do you listen to the radio?
4. When do you listen to the radio?

In our group, four people read a newspaper. Three read the newspaper in the morning. One reads the newspaper in the evening.

## 11 Listening

**Number your paper from 1–5. Listen to the conversations and answer the questions.**

> When does Gino read the newspaper?
> YOU HEAR: I have to read the newspaper in the morning.
> I work in the afternoon and at night.
> WRITE: _____ in the morning _____

1. When do the Youngs relax?
2. When does Liz go to the movies?
3. When do Gloria and her mother go to the supermarket?
4. When does Mike listen to music?
5. When do Gino and Cristina go to the pool?

## 12 Presentation

**Talking about age**

**A**
A: How old is Sam?
B: | He's twenty years old. |
 | He's twenty.

**B**
A: How old is Adela?
B: She's about forty.

**C**
A: How old are you?
B: I'm sixteen.

**D**
A: How old are you?
B: I'd rather not say.

## 13 Practice

**Practice with a partner. Take turns asking about the age of the *Intercom 2000* characters.**

1. Gloria / 16
2. Bob / 17
3. Tom / about 40
4. Lisa / 12
5. Ted / 15
6. Elinor / about 45
7. Joyce / 12
8. Sam / 20
9. Howard / about 50
10. Liz / 21

## 14 Reading

***Before You Read***

1. What do children do after school?
2. Do children ages 6-8 do the same things as children ages 9-11?

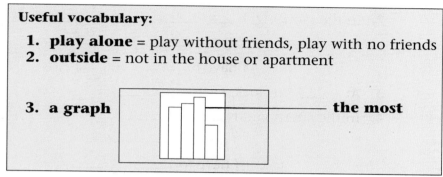

**Useful vocabulary:**

1. **play alone** = play without friends, play with no friends
2. **outside** = not in the house or apartment

3. **a graph**            **the most**

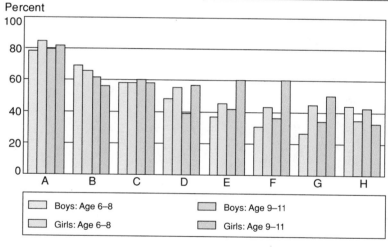

Percent

**KIDS AT PLAY**

KEY:
A. Watch TV
B. Play outside
C. Play with friends at home
D. Do homework
E. Read
F. Talk on the phone
G. Listen to music
H. Play alone at home

Boys: Age 6–8     Boys: Age 9–11

Girls: Age 6–8     Girls: Age 9–11

***After You Read***

**Study the graph and answer the questions.**

1. Who talks on the phone the most?
2. Who listens to music the most?
3. Who plays outside the most?
4. Who reads the most?
5. Who does the most homework?
6. What do many children do? Is this a good activity for children?

## 15 Writing

Choose a day of the week. Complete the first sentence with an adjective.
Complete the other sentences with information about your activities. Write the
sentences in a paragraph and give your paragraph a title.

1. _____Tuesday_____ is a _____ day for me.
2. In the morning, I _____ .
   I don't _____ .
   I have to _____ .
3. At _____ o'clock, I _____ .
4. In the afternoon, I _____ .
   I don't _____ .
   I have to _____ .
5. In the evening, I _____ .
   I don't _____ .

## 16 Final Activity

Work with a partner. Decide which question to ask. One of you asks this question
to half of the class; the other to the other half. Report what you learn to the class.

1. When do you study?
2. Where do you study?
3. When do you clean your house or apartment?
4. When do you read?
5. What do you read?
6. When do you cook?
7. What kind of food do you cook?

**COMMUNICATION**
Inviting and responding to invitations ▪
Describing health problems ▪
Showing concern ▪ Requesting something ▪
Giving and reacting to advice

**GRAMMAR**
*Would you like to* + verb ▪ *Would you get me* + noun ▪ *Should* + verb

## I Don't Feel Well

*It's Saturday afternoon at the Roma. Gino comes out of the kitchen to talk to Cristina.*

GINO: Hey, Cris. Tomorrow's our day off. I have two tickets to the baseball game. Would you like to go?

CRISTINA: Maybe some other time.

GINO: What's the matter? You don't look well.

CRISTINA: I'm getting sick. I ache all over. Mr. Williams told me to go home.

GINO: I'm sorry you don't feel well.

CRISTINA: Me too. And I'm sorry about the game.

GINO: Don't worry about the game. Just go home and take care of yourself. Get some rest. Drink plenty of liquids.

CRISTINA: Yeah. I'm going home right now. Call me after the game. OK?

GINO: Sure. I hope you feel better soon.

CRISTINA: Thanks. I hope so too.

**Inviting someone to do something; accepting and refusing an invitation**

A

| | |
|---|---|
| GINO: | Hey, Cris. I have two tickets to the baseball game. Would you like to go? |
| CRISTINA: | Sorry, Gino. I don't feel well. Maybe some other time. |
| GINO: | OK. I hope you feel better soon. |
| CRISTINA: | Thanks. |

B

| | |
|---|---|
| SEKILA: | Hey, Gloria. I have two tickets to the rock concert. Would you like to go? |
| GLORIA: | Sounds great. |
| SEKILA: | OK. I'll pick you up at 7:00. |
| GLORIA: | See you then. |

2 **Practice**

Work with a partner. Accept or refuse your partner's invitation. Follow the conversation models in *1*.

1. basketball game / sorry
2. baseball game / great
3. rock concert / great
4. movies / sorry

## 3 Interaction

**Work with a partner. Take turns inviting your partner to do something. Your partner accepts or refuses.**

A:  Hey, _____ . I have two tickets to the
_____ . Would you like to go?

B:  Sounds great, _____ .
A:  OK. I'll pick you up at _____ .
B:  See you then.

B:  Sorry, _____ .
I don't feel well. Maybe some other time.
A:  Sure. I hope you feel better soon.
B:  _____ .

## 4 Vocabulary in Context

### Describing health problems; showing concern

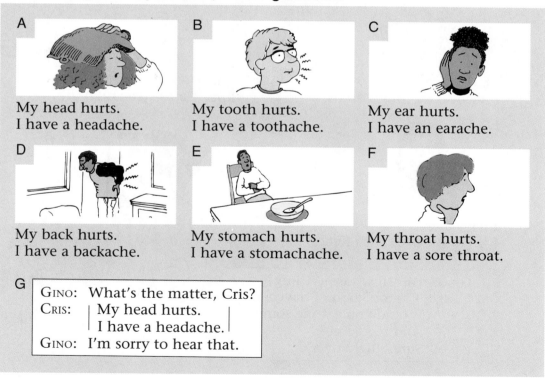

A
My head hurts.
I have a headache.

B
My tooth hurts.
I have a toothache.

C
My ear hurts.
I have an earache.

D
My back hurts.
I have a backache.

E
My stomach hurts.
I have a stomachache.

F
My throat hurts.
I have a sore throat.

G
GINO:  What's the matter, Cris?
CRIS:  My head hurts.
I have a headache.
GINO:  I'm sorry to hear that.

## 5 Practice

Practice with a partner. Take the roles of the people in the pictures in *4*.
Take turns asking what's the matter. Follow the conversation model.

## 6 Presentation

### Describing health problems; requesting something

A

I have a stuffy nose.
I need some nasal spray.

B

I have a headache.
I need some aspirin.

C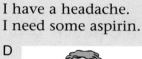

I have a cough.
I need some cough drops.

D

I have a sore throat.
I need some tea and honey.

E

I have a fever.
I need some tea with lemon.

F

GINO: Hi. How's everything?
CRIS: Not too good. I have a cold.
      Would you get me some
      cold medicine?
GINO: Sure. Right away.

## 7 Practice

Practice with a partner. You are at home. You don't feel well. A friend comes to visit. Ask him/her to get you something you need. Follow the conversation model in *6*.

1. cold / orange juice
2. headache / aspirin
3. fever / tea with lemon
4. cough / cough drops
5. cold / tea with lemon

6. sore throat / tea with honey
7. backache / aspirin
8. stuffy nose / nasal spray
9. toothache / aspirin
10. fever / orange juice

## 8 Interaction

Work with a partner. Call a friend and request something.

A: Hi, _____ . This is _____ .
B: Hi. _____ ?
A: Not too good. I have _____ .
   Would you get me some _____ ?
B: Sure. Right away.

## 9 Presentation

Showing concern; giving and reacting to advice

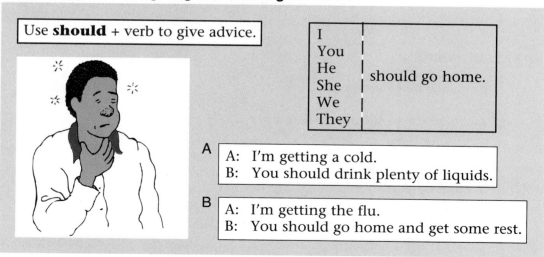

Use **should** + verb to give advice.

| I You He She We They | should go home. |

A
A: I'm getting a cold.
B: You should drink plenty of liquids.

B
A: I'm getting the flu.
B: You should go home and get some rest.

C

| MIKE: | You don't look well, Bob. Are you OK? |
|---|---|
| BOB: | No, I'm not. I have a terrible toothache. |
| MIKE: | Maybe you should go to the dentist. |
| BOB: | Yeah. Maybe I should. |

D

| ELINOR: | You don't look very well, Liz. Are you OK? |
|---|---|
| LIZ: | I'm OK. I'm just tired. |
| ELINOR: | Maybe you should get some rest. |

## 10 Pronunciation

**Pronounce these sentences.**

1. Maybe you should go home.

2. Maybe you should go to the doctor.

3. Maybe you should go to the dentist.

4. Maybe you should drink some tea with lemon.

5. Maybe you should drink some tea with honey.

## 11 Practice

**Work with a partner. Show concern for your partner's condition. He or she will tell you what the matter is. Offer him/her some advice. Follow conversation models C and D in *9*.**

1. have a bad headache / take some aspirin
2. have a toothache / go to the dentist
3. OK: just tired / go home and sleep
4. have an earache / go to the doctor
5. getting a cold / drink some orange juice
6. have a sore throat / drink tea with honey
7. fine: just tired / get some rest
8. getting the flu / go home and sleep

## 12 Interaction

**Work with a partner. Take turns showing concern for your partner's health and giving advice.**

> A: You don't look well, _____ . Are you OK?
> B: No, _____ .
> A: I'm sorry to hear that. Maybe you should _____
> _____ .
> B: Yeah. Maybe I should.

## 13 Listening 

**Number your paper from 1-5. Listen to the conversations and write the letter of the health problem. Three of the eight health problems are extra.**

> YOU HEAR: Excuse me, Mr. Williams. Can I go home?
> I have a terrible headache.
> WRITE:    _a_

a. has a headache
b. has a stomachache
c. has a cough
d. has a sore throat

e. is getting a cold
f. has a backache
g. is getting the flu
h. has a toothache

## 14 Reading

1. Do you take medicine for a headache?
2. What medicine do you take?

---

**Useful vocabulary:**

1. Another word for **ache** is **pain**.
2. **pain relief** = something to stop pain
3. Another word for **doctor** is **physician**.
4. Another word for **medicine** is **drug**.
5. Doctors, nurses, and pharmacists are **health professionals**.
6. **Caution** and **Warning** mean **BE CAREFUL!!!**
7. **adults** (for medicine) = people 12 years old or older
8. **Nursing a baby** means the baby is drinking mother's milk.
9. **seek** = ask for
10. a **pregnant** woman

---

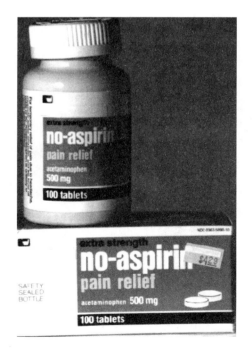

SAFETY
SEALED
BOTTLE

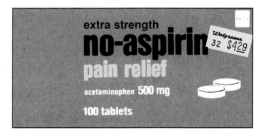

For safe, quick, temporary relief of pain due to headache, muscular aches and pain, and the fever of colds or flu. An effective pain reliever, Acetaminophen is unlikely to cause gastric irritation.
**Directions:** Adults: 1 or 2 tablets 3 or 4 times daily. Use no more than a total of 8 tablets in a 24-hour period or as directed by a physician.
**Caution:** Do not give to children under 12 years of age or use for more than 10 days unless directed by a physician.
**WARNINGS:** AS WITH ANY DRUG, IF YOU ARE PREGNANT OR NURSING A BABY, SEEK THE ADVICE OF A HEALTH PROFESSIONAL BEFORE USING THIS PRODUCT. KEEP THIS AND ALL DRUGS OUT OF REACH OF CHILDREN. IN CASE OF ACCIDENTAL OVERDOSE SEEK PROFESSIONAL ASSISTANCE OR CONTACT A POISON CONTROL CENTER IMMEDIATELY.
Each tablet contains: **Active Ingredient:** Acetaminophen 500 mg. **Other:** Povidone, Starch, Stearic Acid, may also contain Croscarmellose Sodium.

## After You Read

**Read the box and answer the questions.**

1. Does the medicine have aspirin in it?
2. How many tablets are in this package?
3. How much does this package cost?
4. Can adults take 2 tablets at one time?
5. Should they take 12 tablets in one day?
6. Should you give this medicine to an 8-year-old child?

**Complete the advice or warning.**

7. If you are pregnant or nursing a baby, you should talk to a
   _____ before you take this medicine.

## 15 Writing

Lisa is at school. She doesn't feel well. She is going home. She writes a note to her friend, Joyce.

> Joyce,
> I have a bad sore throat. I'm going home. Please call me tonight to give me the homework.
> thanks.
> Lisa

You are at school. You don't feel well. Write a note to a friend. Ask for help. Use Lisa's note as a model.

## 16 Final Activity

A. Everyone in the class has a health problem today. Use your imagination. Decide what your problem is. Move around the classroom and describe your problem to your classmates. Show concern for your classmates and their health problems. Give them advice about what they should do.

B. After five minutes, your teacher tells you to sit down. Write down the names of your classmates and their problems. How many do you remember?

# UNIT 13

**COMMUNICATION**
Talking about the past ▪ Talking about the seasons and the weather ▪ Expressing likes and dislikes ▪ Asking for and giving reasons

**GRAMMAR**
Past tense of *be* ▪ Adverbs of frequency after *be* ▪ Preposition *in* + the seasons and months ▪ *Like* + noun; *like to* + verb ▪ Direct object pronoun: *it* ▪ Questions with *why*; answers with *because*

## Introducing Toshio Ito

*Toshio Ito is a flight attendant for World Airlines. Toshio likes his job because he likes to travel and he likes to work with people. Last month he was in South America. He was in Brazil and Colombia. Last week he was in Hong Kong and Tokyo. Right now he is in Winfield at the home of his friends, the Logans.*

SAM: How was the flight, Toshio?

TOSHIO: Difficult. The weather was bad, and we were late getting into San Francisco. I'm sure the passengers weren't happy about that flight!

LISA: Mr. Ito, do you like your job?

TOSHIO: Sure, Lisa. Today was just a bad day.

LISA: Why do you like it?

TOSHIO: I like to work with people, and I like to travel.

LISA: What's your favorite place?

TOSHIO: That's a hard question. I like South America. I go to Colombia and Brazil a lot. The people are very nice, and I like the weather there. It's always warm. Of course, I like the United States too. New York is nice in the summer, but I don't like it in the winter.

LISA: Why not?

TOSHIO: It's too cold. I hate cold weather.

LISA: I love winter. I love to ice skate.

TOSHIO: A lot of my friends like to skate too, Lisa, but not me.

# 1 Presentation

## Talking about the past

| I<br>He<br>She | was | |
|---|---|---|
| We<br>You<br>They | were | in New York yesterday. |

1. Toshio Ito was in South America last month.
2. Last week he was in Hong Kong and Tokyo.

3. Nhu Trinh was in California last week.
4. Yesterday she was in New York.

**Useful expressions:**

| yesterday | | last night | |
|---|---|---|---|
| yesterday | morning<br>afternoon<br>evening | last | week<br>weekend<br>Sunday<br>month<br>summer<br>year |

| Name | Yesterday | Last week | Last month |
|------|-----------|-----------|------------|
| Toshio | Winfield | Hong Kong, Tokyo | Brazil, Colombia |
| Nhu Trinh | New York | California | Hong Kong, Tokyo |
| the Logans | Winfield | Winfield | New York City |
| the Youngs | Winfield | Boston | New York City |

**Look at the chart. Make statements about where the people were. Another student will accept or correct the statement.**

> The Logans / New York City / last month
> A:  The Logans were in New York City last month.
> B:  That's right.
>
> Toshio / Hong Kong / yesterday
> A:  Toshio was in Hong Kong yesterday.
> B:  No.  He was in Winfield.

1. Nhu Trinh / Boston / yesterday
2. The Logans / Winfield / last week
3. Toshio / Hong Kong / last month
4. The Youngs / Winfield / last week
5. Toshio / South America / last month
6. The Logans / Hong Kong / yesterday
7. Nhu Trinh / California / yesterday
8. The Logans / New York City / last month
9. Toshio / Brazil / last week
10. The Youngs / Boston / yesterday

## 3 Interaction

**Find out where five of your classmates were yesterday and last week. Report to the class.**

> A:  I was _____  _____ . What about you?
> B:  I was _____ .

## 4 Vocabulary in Context

### Talking about the seasons and the weather

> Use **in** + **(the)** + seasons.
> Use **in** + months.

**Useful vocabulary:**

autumn = fall

**A**

March, April, and May are **spring** months in New York.

A: What's the weather like in the spring?
B: It's **warm**.

**B**

June, July, and August are **summer** months in New York.

A: What's the weather like in the summer?
B: It's **hot**.

**C**

September, October, and November are **fall** months in New York.

A: What's the weather like in fall?
B: It's **cool**.

**D**

December, January, and February are **winter** months in New York.

A: What's the weather like in winter?
B: It's **cold**.

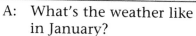

A: What's the weather like in January?
B: It's **cold**.

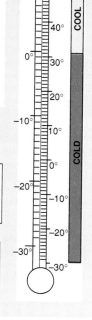

Celsius / Fahrenheit

HOT
WARM
COOL
COLD

## 5 Practice

**Work with a partner.  Take turns asking about the weather in New York.**

1. fall
2. spring
3. winter
4. summer

5. January
6. May
7. July
8. October

## 6 Presentation

**Talking about normal weather patterns**

1. It's **always** hot in San Juan in the summer.
2. It's **usually** warm in New York in the spring.
3. It's **sometimes** cool in New York in September.
4. It's **almost never** hot in New York in October.
5. It's **never** hot in New York in the winter.

A:   Is it hot in ____your city____ in the winter?
B:   No, it isn't.  It's never hot in the winter.

A:   Is it cool in ____your city____ in the spring?
B:   Yes, it is.  It's usually cool.

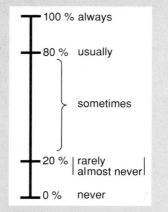

## 7 Pronunciation

**Repeat these sentences.**

1. It's warm in Brazil.

   It's always warm in Brazil.

2. It's hot in New York.

   It's hot in New York in the summer.

   It's usually hot in New York in the summer.

## 8 Practice

**Work with a partner. Take turns asking questions about the weather where you live. Use the conversation models in 6.**

1. hot / winter
2. cool / summer
3. cold / fall
4. warm / spring

5. hot / fall
6. warm / winter
7. cool / summer
8. cold / spring

## 9 Interaction

**Make a list of cities and towns you know. Exchange lists with a partner. Ask your partner about the weather in the places on his/her list.**

> A: What's the weather like in _____ in _____ ?
> B: It's always _____ .

## 10 Presentation

### Expressing likes and dislikes

| **Like + *noun*** | **Like to + *verb*** |
| --- | --- |
| I like winter. | |
| I like cold weather. | I like to skate. |
| I like summer. | |
| I like hot weather. | I like to go to the beach. |

A

A: Do you like winter?
B: Yes, I do.
A: What do you like to do in winter?
B: I like to skate.

B

A: Do you like November?
B: No, I don't.

## 11 Practice

Practice with a partner. Find out if he/she likes the seasons: spring, summer, fall, winter. If he/she says *yes*, find out what he/she likes to do. Report back to the class.

> REPORT: Marina likes summer. She likes to swim in the summer. She doesn't like winter.

## 12 Presentation

**Asking for and giving reasons**

A

Do you like winter? I hate **it.**

| INTERVIEWER: | Do you like winter? |
|---|---|
| TOSHIO: | No, I don't. I hate it. |
| INTERVIEWER: | Why do you hate it? |
| TOSHIO: | Because I don't like cold weather. |

B

| INTERVIEWER: | Do you like January? |
|---|---|
| LISA: | January is my favorite month. I love it. |
| INTERVIEWER: | Why do you like it? |
| LISA: | Because I like to ice skate. |

## 13 Interaction

Make a small group. Find out what seasons or months are the favorites in your group and why.

> A: What's your favorite _____ ?
> B: _____ .
> A: Why do you like it?
> B: Because _____ .
> A: What do you like to do in _____ ?
> B: I like to _____ .

**Number your paper from 1-5. Listen to the conversations and find out why or why not. Write the letter of the correct reason on your paper.**

> Gloria likes Winfield because ___a___ .
> **a.** it's pretty
> **b.** it's near New York
> **c.** it's small

1. Lisa likes her English class because ____ .
   **a.** she likes to read and write
   **b.** her teacher is interesting
   **c.** they read interesting books
2. Tom likes to travel because ____ .
   **a.** he sees new places
   **b.** he meets interesting people
   **c.** he likes to learn new things
3. Liz doesn't like to cook because ____ .
   **a.** the kitchen is hot
   **b.** she doesn't like to clean the kitchen
   **c.** she doesn't have a good kitchen
4. Mike doesn't like winter because ____ .
   **a.** he can't play tennis
   **b.** he can't run
   **c.** he can't swim
5. Joyce likes fall because ____ .
   **a.** it's pretty
   **b.** she likes school
   **c.** it's cool

**15** Writing

**Write a short paragraph about your favorite season. Answer these questions in your paragraph.**

1. What is your favorite season?
2. Why do you like it?
3. What do you like to do in that season?

## 16 Reading

### Before You Read

1. Do you know where Brazil is?
2. Do you know the name of its capital city?

**Useful vocabulary:**

1. **capital**: Washington, D.C., is the capital of the United States.
2. **coast**: Rio de Janeiro is on the Atlantic coast.
3. **interior**: Brasília is in the interior of Brazil.
4. **site** = place or location
5. **plans, master plan** = drawings, the big or complete plan

### Brasília

Brasília is the new, modern capital of Brazil, the largest country in South America and the fifth largest country in the world. The old capital was Rio de Janeiro on the Atlantic coast.

At the time of its construction, the idea for a new capital city was not new. In 1789, and again in 1822, people talked about a new capital in the interior of the country. In 1957 the site and the plans were ready. Lúcio Costa drew the master plan, and world-famous Brazilian architect Oscar Niemeyer was the architect of the major buildings. In 1960 the new city was opened, but it was not completed for many years.

Brasília is located in a state named Goiás, about 600 miles (960 kilometers) north and west of Rio de Janeiro. It is at an altitude of 3,500 feet (1,100 meters). The climate of Brasília is warm and dry, and the weather is usually very good. It is usually warm during the day. At night it is sometimes cool. It is never very cold or very hot. The temperature varies between 81°F (27°C) and 57°F (14°C). It is very dry from March to October.

*After You Read*

**Read the sentences. Say *That's right*, *That's wrong*, or *I don't know*.**

1. Brasília is the new capital of Brazil.
2. The old capital city was in the interior of Brazil.
3. The architect of the major buildings was Brazilian.
4. Lúcio Costa was Brazilian.
5. It's sometimes cold in Brasília.

6. It rains  from March to October in Brasília.

## 17 Final Activity

**This is an activity for the entire class. Copy the form below. The object of this activity is to fill in all the blanks on the form with the names of students in your class. Move around the class, and ask questions. When a student answers *Yes*, write in his or her name.**

Tim, do you like to skate?

Yes, I do.

---

**FIND SOMEONE WHO...**

1. ...likes to skate   *Tim*
2. ...was at the beach last summer
3. ...has a nickname
4. ...likes very hot weather
5. ...was at home last night
6. ...likes February
7. ...likes Italian food
8. ...doesn't like summer

---

COMMUNICATION
Talking about activities in the past ▪
Talking about where and when people
were born

GRAMMAR
Past of *be*: yes/no questions, Wh-questions,
and short answers ▪ Irregular pasts: *went,
met, saw, had* ▪ *Be born*

# How Was Your Weekend?

*It's Monday afternoon and Toshio Ito is on his way to Kennedy Airport. His flight
leaves for Japan at 7:30 PM. He's talking to Nhu Trinh, another flight attendant
for World Airlines. She is Vietnamese. She was born in Vietnam. She lives in San
Francisco now.*

TRINH:   How was your weekend, Toshio?

TOSHIO:   It was nice. I went to visit some friends in Winfield. We went to a
basketball game at the high school and to a concert. I met a lot of
their friends. What about you? Were you in New York City all
weekend?

TRINH:   Yes, I was. I went to a movie. I saw "Summer to Remember."
It was awful.

TOSHIO:   That's too bad. Next time we're both in New York for a weekend,
you should come to Winfield with me.

## 1 Presentation

### Asking about the past

| Was | I<br>he<br>she<br>it | in New York? | Yes, | I<br>he<br>she<br>it | was. | No, | I<br>he<br>she<br>it | wasn't. |
|---|---|---|---|---|---|---|---|---|
| Were | we<br>you<br>they | | | we<br>you<br>they | were. | | we<br>you<br>they | weren't. |

**A**
A: Was Nhu Trinh in New York City all weekend?
B: Yes, she was.

**B**
A: Was she in the hotel all weekend?
B: No, she wasn't.

**C**
A: Were you in school yesterday?
B: No, I wasn't. I was sick.

## 2 Practice

| Name | Last weekend | Last summer | Last December |
|---|---|---|---|
| Toshio Ito | Winfield | Brazil | Tokyo |
| Nhu Trinh | New York City | California | Tokyo |
| the Riveras | Winfield | New York City | New York City |
| the Youngs | Winfield | at the beach | Winfield |

Look at the chart. With a partner, ask and answer questions about where the people were last weekend, last summer, and last December.

1. Nhu Trinh / New York City / last weekend
2. the Riveras / in Winfield / last summer
3. the Youngs / in Winfield / last December
4. Toshio Ito / in Tokyo / last weekend
5. the Youngs / at the beach / last summer
6. the Riveras / in New York City / last weekend
7. Nhu Trinh / Brazil / last weekend
8. Toshio Ito / Tokyo / last December
9. the Youngs / Winfield / last summer
10. Nhu Trinh / California / last weekend

## 3 Practice

Look at the chart in 2. Make correct and incorrect statements about where the people were. Your partner will correct you if you make an incorrect statement.

> A:  Nhu Trinh was in Boston last summer.
> B:  No, she wasn't. She was in California.
>
> A:  The Riveras were in Winfield last weekend.
> B:  Yes, they were.

## 4 Interaction

Write the names of five friends or family members on a piece of paper. Exchange lists with a partner. Find out where the people were yesterday, last Saturday, and last Sunday. Find out where your partner was, too.

> A:  *Was Steve* _____ *at home* _____ yesterday?
> B:  *No, he wasn't. He was in Boston.*

## 5 Listening

Number your paper from 1-10. Listen to the sentence and write *in the past* or *now*.

> YOU HEAR:  Bob's at a basketball game.
> WRITE:  now

## 6 Presentation

**Talking about where and when people were born**

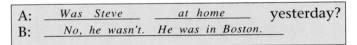

> I was born **in** New York.
> I was born **in** July.
> I was born **in** 1975.
> BUT
> I was born **on** July 15, 1968.

> Use **on** when you give the full date.

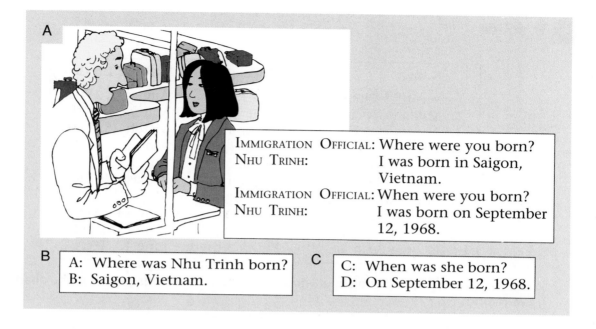

A

IMMIGRATION OFFICIAL: Where were you born?
NHU TRINH:           I was born in Saigon, Vietnam.
IMMIGRATION OFFICIAL: When were you born?
NHU TRINH:           I was born on September 12, 1968.

B
A: Where was Nhu Trinh born?
B: Saigon, Vietnam.

C
C: When was she born?
D: On September 12, 1968.

## 7 Pronunciation

**Repeat these questions.**

1. Were you born in Brazil?
2. Where were you born?
3. Were you in California last summer?
4. Where were you last summer?

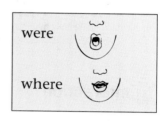

| were | |
| where | |

## 8 Listening

**Number your paper from 1-8. Listen to each date and write the letter of the one you hear.**

1. **a.** June 20, 1960
   **b.** June 20, 1916
2. **a.** January 1, 1968
   **b.** January 1, 1978
3. **a.** May 21, 1953
   **b.** May 31, 1953
4. **a.** December 12, 1980
   **b.** December 12, 1918

5. **a.** November 25, 1934
   **b.** November 26, 1934
6. **a.** July 20, 1992
   **b.** July 20, 1982
7. **a.** February 5, 1971
   **b.** February 15, 1971
8. **a.** September 2, 1957
   **b.** December 2, 1957

## 9 Practice

| | Name | Place of Birth | Date of Birth |
|---|---|---|---|
| 1. | Whitney Houston | New Jersey | August 9, 1963 |
| 2. | Mikhail Gorbachev | Soviet Union | March 2, 1931 |
| 3. | Sandra Day O'Connor | Arizona | March 26, 1930 |
| 4. | Princess Stephanie | Monaco | February 1, 1965 |
| 5. | Carl Lewis | Alabama | July 1, 1961 |
| 6. | Michael Jackson | Indiana | August 29, 1958 |
| 7. | Liza Minnelli | California | March 12, 1946 |
| 8. | Steffi Graf | Germany | June 14, 1969 |
| 9. | Benazir Bhutto | Pakistan | June 21, 1953 |
| 10. | George Bush | Massachusetts | June 12, 1924 |

**Ask and answer questions about where and when the famous people in the chart were born.**

> A: Where was Whitney Houston born?
> B: She was born in New Jersey.
> A: When was she born?
> B: On August 9, 1963.

## 10 Interaction

**Work with a partner. Take turns being the immigration official and practice the conversation in *6*, page 135. Use personal information.**

## 11 Presentation

**Talking about the past**

A
> Toshio was in Winfield last weekend.
> He **met** the Logans' friends.
> He **went** to a basketball game and to a concert.
> He **had** a nice weekend.

B
> Nhu Trinh was in New York City last weekend.
> She **went** to a movie.
> She **saw** "Summer to Remember."

C

| TRINH: | How was your weekend, Toshio? |
| --- | --- |
| TOSHIO: | It was nice.  I went to Winfield. How was *your* weekend, Trinh? |
| TRINH: | Not too good.  I went to a movie.  It was awful. |

| Present | Past* |
| --- | --- |
| go/goes | went |
| meet/meets | met |
| see/sees | saw |
| have/has | had |

*One form for all pronouns

## 12 Practice

**Talk about what the following people did.   Imagine whom they met or what they saw.**

Toshio / Rome / last month
A:   Toshio went to Rome last month.
B:   He met some nice people.
      He saw some old buildings.

1. Trinh / Tokyo / last month
2. Gino and Cristina / New York City / last weekend
3. The Youngs / Washington, D.C. / last year
4. Sekila / library / yesterday
5. Toshio / Brazil / last month
6. The Logans / the beach / last summer
7. Mrs. Rivera / Puerto Rico / last summer
8. Bob and Mike / rock concert / last month
9. Dr. Young / hospital / yesterday
10. Lisa and Joyce / pool / last weekend

## 13 Interaction

**Talk about last weekend.**

A:   How was your weekend, _____ ?
B:   _____ . I _____ .
      How was *your* weekend?
A:   _____ . I _____ .

## 14 Reading

### Before You Read

1. How often do you write letters? Whom do you write to?
2. Do you write letters to say thank you?

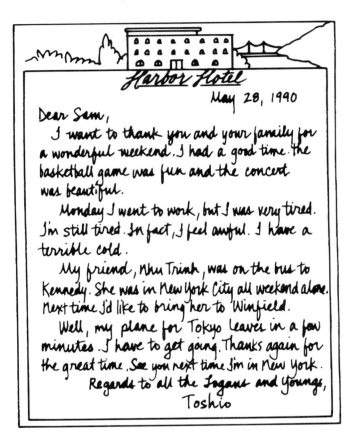

Harbor Hotel

May 28, 1990

Dear Sam,

I want to thank you and your family for a wonderful weekend. I had a good time. The basketball game was fun and the concert was beautiful.

Monday I went to work, but I was very tired. I'm still tired. In fact, I feel awful. I have a terrible cold.

My friend, Nhu Trinh, was on the bus to Kennedy. She was in New York City all weekend alone. Next time I'd like to bring her to Winfield.

Well, my plane for Tokyo leaves in a few minutes. I have to get going. Thanks again for the great time. See you next time I'm in New York.

Regards to all the Logans and Youngs,
Toshio

### After You Read

**Read the question. Say *That's right*, *That's wrong*, or *I don't know*.**

1. Toshio is in San Francisco.
2. Toshio was with Nhu Trinh on the bus to Kennedy Airport.
3. Nhu Trinh was with Toshio on the plane to San Francisco.
4. Toshio is sick.
5. Toshio is writing during the flight to Japan.
6. Toshio is coming to Winfield soon.

## 15 Writing

Imagine you visited a friend for the weekend.  Write a short thank you note to them.  Use the first and last paragraphs of Toshio's letter as a model.

## 16 Reentry

Complete the sentences with the correct form of *be*: *am, is, are, was, were.*

1. Winfield _____ a nice, small city.
2. Toshio _____ in Winfield last weekend.
3. Sam Logan _____ Toshio's friend.
4. The Logans _____ at home last weekend.
5. Toshio _____ at their house for dinner last night.
6. I _____ Nhu Trinh.
7. I _____ born in Vietnam.
8. My mother and father _____ in San Francisco now.
9. Toshio Ito _____ my friend.
10. We _____ flight attendants for World Airlines.

## 17 Final Activity

A. Complete these sentences.  Write them on a piece of paper and give them to your teacher.

I was _____ last night.
I was _____ last weekend.
I was born on _____ .

B. Your teacher will give you someone else's paper.  Move around the class and ask questions that begin with *Were you...?* to find out whose paper you have.

C. When you find the correct person, ask where he or she was born.

# UNIT 15

**COMMUNICATION**
Talking about plans ▪ Talking about family relationships ▪ Talking about marital status

**GRAMMAR**
Present continuous with future meaning ▪ Future time indicators *next* vs. *this* ▪ *has to* + verb

# What Are You Doing This Weekend?

*Pablo and Melanie Nava live in Mexico City. Pablo is Mexican, and Melanie is American. Melanie is an English teacher. She was born in California, and her parents still live there. Twenty-two years ago, she went to Mexico City to teach English. She met Pablo Nava, a young architect, there. They were married two years later. Their children were born in Mexico. Carlos is 18, and Ana is 14. Pablo's mother is a widow and lives with them.*

*The Navas are going to the United States next month. First they are going to California to visit Melanie's mother and father. Then they are going to the Grand Canyon, Santa Fe, Washington, D.C., and New York. In New York, they are visiting Mike Young and his family in Winfield. Mike lived with them in Mexico City last summer.*

*It's Friday evening. The Navas are having dinner.*

MELANIE: What are your plans for the weekend, Pablo?

PABLO: I have to go to the office tomorrow morning. I have a lot of work. What about you, dear?

MELANIE: I have to go to the travel agent. What are you doing this weekend, Carlos? Can you help me clean the house?

CARLOS: I guess so, but I have to study for my exams, too. I'm going over to Luisa's house tomorrow afternoon.

MELANIE: What about you, Ana?

ANA: I have a dentist appointment, but I'd like to go to the travel agent with you. I want to answer Mike's letter, too.

**140**     **Unit Fifteen**

**Talking about future plans**

Use the present continuous + a future time expression to talk about future plans.

**Useful expressions:**

**Next** means the coming one.

next Tuesday
next week
next month
next June
next summer
next year

You are here.

This week

Next week

| June | | | | | | |
|---|---|---|---|---|---|---|
| Su | M | T | W | Th | F | S |
| | ☆1 | 2 | 3 | 4 | 5 | 6 |
| 7 | 8 | 9 | 10 | 11 | 12 | 13 |
| 14 | 15 | 16 | 17 | 18 | 19 | 20 |
| 21 | 22 | 23 | 24 | 25 | 26 | 27 |
| 28 | 29 | 30 | | | | |

A: Where are the Navas going?
B: To the United States.
A: When are they going?
B: Next month.

**2** Practice

Take turns asking and answering questions about the future plans of the *Intercom 2000* characters. Follow the conversation model in *1*.

| Who | Where | When |
|---|---|---|
| 1. the Navas | United States | next month |
| 2. Ted | New York City | next weekend |
| 3. the Logans | beach | next summer |
| 4. Cristina | Colombia | next December |
| 5. Tom Logan | Boston | next week |
| 6. Gino and Cristina | New York City | next Monday |

## 3 Presentation

**Talking about plans for this week**

| Day | Week | | Tomorrow | |
|---|---|---|---|---|
| today | this | week | tomorrow | morning |
| this   morning | | weekend | | afternoon |
|      afternoon | this | Friday | | evening |
|      evening | | Saturday afternoon | | night |
| tonight | | | | |

**This** means the present one.

**A**

A: What are Ana and Melanie doing tomorrow?
B: They're going to the travel agent.

**B**

A: What is Carlos doing tonight?
B: He's going out with friends.

**C**

A: What are you doing this weekend?
B: Nothing much. I'm staying home.
A: Well, have a nice weekend.
B: OK. You too.

## 4 Practice

**Work with a partner. Take turns asking and answering questions about plans for this week. Follow conversation models A and B in 3.**

1. Dr. Young / tonight  (work)
2. Ted / Friday evening  (stay home)
3. the Logans / this Saturday (clean the house)
4. Gino and Cristina / this Saturday  (work)
5. Gloria / this weekend (play tennis with Bob)
6. Sam / Saturday (go out with a friend)
7. Joyce and Lisa / Saturday afternoon (go to the movies)
8. Sam and Bob / Saturday afternoon (study)
9. Tom and Adela / Saturday evening (go out with friends)
10. Mrs. Rivera / weekend (stay home)

## 5 Interaction

**Say goodbye to your classmates before the weekend.**

> A: What are you doing _____ ?
> B: I'm _____ .
> A: Well, have a _____ .
> B: _____ . You too.

## 6 Listening

**Number your paper from 1-4. Listen to the conversations and find out what the people are doing and when. Choose from the information provided.**

> YOU HEAR:  MIKE:  What are you doing this weekend, Bob?
>            BOB:   I'm playing tennis with Gloria on Sunday.
>
> WRITE:     Bob and Gloria are ____playing tennis on Sunday____ .
>
>            · playing tennis       · on Saturday
>            · going swimming       · on Sunday

**1.** Adela and Tom are _____ .

· going to the movies     · tonight
· going out for dinner     · tomorrow night

**2.** Joyce is _____ .

· helping her mother     · Saturday morning
· going to a movie       · Saturday afternoon

**3.** Gino and Cristina are _____ .

· going to a museum      · next Sunday
· going to a movie       · next Monday

**4.** Mike is _____ .

· going to the movies     · Friday night
· studying                · Saturday night

### More family relationships

These are the members of the Nava family.

1. Maria is Pablo's mother and Ana's **grandmother**.
2. Joseph is Melanie's father and Carlos's **grandfather**.
3. Carlos and Ana are Pablo and Melanie's children and Maria's **grandchildren**.
4. Julia, Joseph, and Maria are Ana's **grandparents**.
5. Carlos is Julia's **grandson**; Ana is her **granddaughter**.

## 8 Practice

**Identify these people by their relationship to each other.**

> Julia — Melanie
> Julia is Melanie's mother.

1. Maria — Ana
2. Joseph — Carlos
3. Ana — Joseph
4. Carlos — Julia
5. Carlos and Ana — Julia

6. Julia and Joseph — Carlos
7. Julia — Ana
8. Carlos and Ana — Pablo
9. Ana — Carlos
10. Maria and Julia — Ana

## 9 Practice

**Give two identifications for each person. Several answers are correct.**

> Ana
>
> Ana is Carlos's sister.
> Ana is Julia's granddaughter.

1. Maria
2. Pablo
3. Melanie

4. Joseph
5. Julia
6. Carlos

## 10 Reentry

**Talking about family**

**Complete the sentences with the correct possessive adjective:**
*my, his, her, our, their.*

1. I'm Julia Kansky. _____ husband's name is Joseph.
2. We have two sons and a daughter. _____ daughter's name is Melanie. _____ sons are Paul and Robert.
3. Melanie is married. _____ husband's name is Pablo Nava.
4. Pablo and Melanie have two children. _____ names are Carlos and Ana.
5. Pablo's father is dead. _____ wife is a widow. _____ name is Maria Gomez de Nava.

## 11 Reentry

### Age

**Practice with a partner. Take turns asking about the age of Melanie's relatives.**

> A: How old is Carlos?
> B: He's 18.

## 12 Presentation

### Talking about marital status and family

A

We're married. We met in Mexico City. We were married there, too.

Pablo and Melanie

B

I'm single.

Carlos

**Useful vocabulary:**

widowed
  a widow (*female*)
  a widower (*male*)
divorced

C
> A: Are you married?
> B: No, I'm single.
> A: Do you have any brothers and sisters?
> B: Yes, I have two. One brother and one sister.
> A: What are their names?
> B: Maria Elena and Juan.

D
> A: Are you married?
> B: Yes, I am.
> A: Do you have any children?
> B: Yes, I have three. Two boys and a girl.
> A: What are their names and how old are they?
> B: Marta is 12, Manuel is 10, and Tito is 7.

## 13 Interaction

Talk about your marital status and your family.

A: Are you married?

B: Yes, I am.
A: Do you have any children?
B: _Yes, I do_ .
   _Two. A girl and a boy_ .
A: What are their names and how old are they?
B: _Ana is 4 and Pablito is 2_ .

B: No, I'm not.
A: Do you have any brothers and sisters?
B: _Yes, I do_ . _One sister_ .
A: What is _her_ name?
B: _Sara_ .

## 14 Presentation

### Expressing obligations

1. Pablo has to go to the office.
2. Melanie has to clean the house.

| He | has to study. |
| She | |

A: What is Pablo doing this weekend?
B: He has to go to the office.

## 15 Pronunciation

**Repeat these sentences.**

1. Pablo has to work.
2. Melanie has to go to the travel agent.
3. Ana has to go to the dentist.
4. Carlos and Ana have to study.
5. Melanie, Ana, and Carlos have to clean the house.

has to = /hæstə/

have to = /hæftə/

## 16 Practice

Look at the chart. Ask and answer questions about what each person is doing this weekend. Follow the conversation model in *14*.

| This Weekend | | | |
|---|---|---|---|
| **Pablo** | go to the office<br>finish a lot of work<br>wash the car | **Carlos** | study<br>help his mother<br>wash the car |
| **Melanie** | go to the travel agent<br>go to the doctor<br>clean the house | **Ana** | go to the dentist<br>go to the travel agent<br>write a letter |

## 17 Reading

*Before You Read*

1. Do you write letters before you visit people?
2. What information do you give in the letter?

Dear Mike,

We were all happy to get your letter. Yes, we're coming to New York, believe it or not. I'm so excited. First we're going to Los Angeles to visit my grandmother and grandfather for a week. Then we're driving to the Grand Canyon and Santa Fe in their car. After Santa Fe, they're going back to Los Angeles, and we're flying to Washington for four days. From Washington, we're taking the train to NY. We're arriving in New York on July 20th. I hope you can meet us at the station. If not, we can find our way to Winfield. Hope you are all well. See you in a month.

Love, Ana

**Read the statement and say** *That's right, That's wrong,* **or** *I don't know.*

1. Ana has a letter from Mike.
2. The Navas are taking the train to the Grand Canyon.
3. Ana's grandparents are not going to New York.
4. The Navas are staying in Santa Fe for a week.
5. The Youngs are meeting the Navas in New York.

## 18 Writing

Write a short letter to a friend. Thank him or her for an invitation to visit. Tell him or her when you are arriving. Use Ana's letter as a model.

## 19 Final Activity

> **Useful language:**
>
> A: Can you go to the movies Friday night?
> B: No, I can't. I have to babysit for my Aunt Mary.

A. Copy the chart below. Write down the things you have to do this weekend.

B. Now, plan one activity with a partner for a time when you are both free. Then, tell the class about your plans for the weekend. Talk about what you *have* to do and what you *want* to do with your partner.

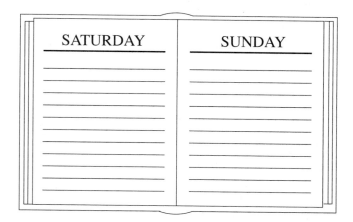

**COMMUNICATION**
Talking about school ▪ Congratulating ▪
Talking about clothes ▪ Talking about colors ▪
Making a purchase

**GRAMMAR**
Questions: What color? What size?

# Buying a Gift

*It's June and the end of the school year in Winfield.*

BOB: Sorry I'm late, Mike.
MIKE: That's OK. How was your geometry exam?
BOB: Not bad. I'm sure I did well.
MIKE: Congratulations! I have some good news, too. The Navas are coming in July.
BOB: Great! ...So, what do you want to do now?
MIKE: I want to go buy a gift for my dad. His birthday is this weekend.
BOB: Why don't we try Allen's? They have great men's clothes.

CLERK: Good afternoon. May I help you?
MIKE: Yes. I'm looking for a shirt for my father.
CLERK: What size?
MIKE: Large.
CLERK: This way, please. What color would you like?
MIKE: His favorite colors are blue and green.

BOB: How about this one, Mike? It has a good combination of blue and green.
MIKE: Yeah. I like it. How much is it?
CLERK: $29.95.
MIKE: OK. I'll take it.
CLERK: Would you like it gift wrapped?
MIKE: Yes, please.

## 1 Presentation

**Talking about school**

**A**

$$4x^2 + 4y^2 = 25$$

algebra

**B**

geometry

**C**

biology

**D**

He , $H_2O$ , Fe , Ca

chemistry

**E**

physics

**F**

history

**G**

| | |
|---|---|
| MIKE: | How was your geometry exam? |
| BOB: | Not bad.  I'm sure I did well! |
| MIKE: | Congratulations! |

**H**

| | |
|---|---|
| GLORIA: | How was your Spanish exam? |
| JUDY: | Hard.  I hope I passed. |
| GLORIA: | I hope so, too. |

## 2 Interaction

**Take turns asking your partner about an exam.  Use the conversation models in *1*.**

A: How was your _____ exam?

B: _____ . _____ .

A: _____ .

## 3 Vocabulary in Context

### Talking about clothes

| A: | What's the little girl wearing? |
| B: | She's wearing a dress, shoes, and socks. |

## 4 Practice

Work with a partner. Take turns asking and answering questions about what the people in *3* are wearing.

## 5 Presentation

### Talking about colors

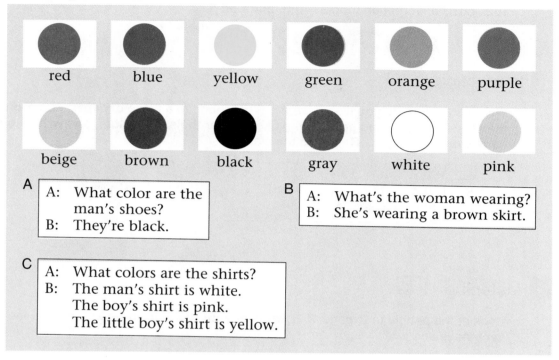

red   blue   yellow   green   orange   purple

beige   brown   black   gray   white   pink

A
A: What color are the man's shoes?
B: They're black.

B
A: What's the woman wearing?
B: She's wearing a brown skirt.

C
A: What colors are the shirts?
B: The man's shirt is white.
The boy's shirt is pink.
The little boy's shirt is yellow.

## 6 Pronunciation

**Repeat these sentences.**

1. The woman is wearing a skirt.

   The woman is wearing a brown skirt.

2. The boy is wearing a shirt.

   The boy is wearing a pink shirt.

3. The girl is wearing jeans.

   The girl is wearing blue jeans.

## 7 Practice

Work with a partner. Take turns asking about the color of the clothing in *3*, page 152. Use conversation models A, B, and C in *5*.

## 8 Interaction

What two colors do you like to wear? Write them on a piece of paper. Go around the classroom and find people who like to wear the same colors, and write their names on your paper. Report to the class.

> A: What colors do you like to wear?
> B: I like to wear _____ and _____ . What about you?
> A: I like to wear _____ and _____ .

## 9 Listening 🔊

Look at the people in *3*, page 152. Number your paper from 1-10. Listen to the sentences and write *yes* or *no*.

> YOU HEAR: The man is wearing a brown suit.
> WRITE: _no_

## 10 Presentation 🔊

Making a purchase

| | Sizes | | | |
|---|---|---|---|---|
| | **small** | **medium** | **large** | **extra large** |
| **Shirts, Blouses** | S | M | L | XL |
| **Men's pants** | 28-30 | 32-34 | 36-38 | 40-42 |
| **Women's pants and dresses** | 6-8 | 10-12 | 14-16 | 18 |

**Useful vocabulary:**

a pair of jeans
2 pairs of pants
    slacks
    shorts
    shoes
    sandals
    socks

CLERK: Good afternoon. May I help you?
MIKE: Yes. I'm looking for a pair of pants.
CLERK: What size?
MIKE: 34.
CLERK: This way, please. What color would you like?
MIKE: Gray.

## 11 Practice

Practice with a partner. Take turns being the clerk and the customer. Use the conversation model in *10* and the information below.

1. shirt / medium / blue
2. a pair of shorts / 40 / red
3. a pair of jeans / 32 / black
4. blouse / large / white
5. skirt / 12 / brown

6. a pair of pants / 6 / blue
7. blouse / large / yellow
8. T-shirt / extra large / green
9. a pair of shorts / 14 / pink
10. a pair of jeans / 10 / white

## 12 Interaction

Work with a partner. Take turns making a purchase.

CLERK: Good _____ . May I help you?
CUSTOMER: Yes. I'm looking for _____ .
CLERK: What size?
CUSTOMER: _____ .
CLERK: This way, please. What color would you like?
CUSTOMER: _____ .

## 13 Presentation

### Completing the purchase

CLERK: How about this shirt?
CUSTOMER: I like it. How much is it?
CLERK: $29.95.
CUSTOMER: I'll take it.

## 14 Interaction

**Complete the purchase for a shirt, tie, skirt, or blouse.**

A: How about this _____ ?
B: I like it. How much is it?
A: _____ .
B: I'll take it.

## 15 Reading

### Before You Read

1. What kind of advertisements do you find in magazines and newspapers?
2. When do people order things by mail?

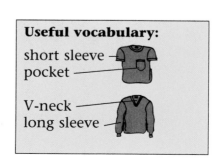

**Useful vocabulary:**

short sleeve
pocket

V-neck
long sleeve

*After You Read*

**Answer these questions with information from the ad.**

1. What are the name, address, and telephone number of the T-shirt company?
2. Do all four styles come in 12 colors?
3. Does the long-sleeved T-shirt come in light green?
4. How much do two short-sleeved T-shirts cost?
5. What is the style number of the T-shirt with a pocket?
6. If you want a beige T-shirt, what styles can you order?

## 16 Writing

**Imagine you have $25. Decide which T-shirts to order. Complete the order blank appropriately.**

**DAYTIME PHONE**
(in case we have a question about your order)     Area Code (     )

| SATISFACTION GUARANTEED! | Style Description | Style No. | Size | Color No. | Quantity (No. of items, sets, or pairs, not packages) | Amount |
|---|---|---|---|---|---|---|
| | | | | | | • |
| | | | | | | • |
| | | | | | | • |
| | | | | | | • |
| | | | | | | • |
| | | | | | | • |
| | | | | | | • |

**PAYMENT METHOD**
☐ Check or Money Order enclosed. ☐ master card ☐ VISA

CREDIT CARD NUMBER:     ($15.00 minimum credit card order, please.)

MONTH  —  YEAR     Please do not leave spaces between numbers

Card Expiration Date          Credit Card Customer Signature

**CALL IN YOUR ORDER!**
1-800-657-1234

**SHIPPING & HANDLING**
| Amount Ordered | Add |
|---|---|
| $10.00 and over......$1.60 |
| $10.01 to $20.00.....$2.40 |
| $20.01 to $30.00.....$3.60 |
| $30.01 to $40.00.....$4.70 |
| $40.01 to $50.00.....$6.00 |
| $50.01 and up.........$7.00 |

| Amount Ordered | • |
|---|---|
| Add Sales Tax: CA(6%), NC (5%), TN (7.75) | • |
| Shipping & Handling | • |
| **TOTAL** | • |

## 17 Final Activity

**Write a conversation following these instructions. Practice it with a partner and role play it for the class.**

> A (Clerk):  Greet the customer.
> B:  Respond and say what you are looking for.
> A:  Ask about size.
> B:  Respond.
> A:  Ask about color.
> B:  Respond.
> A:  Show an item and comment on it.
> B:  Ask about price.
> A:  Respond.
> B:  Agree to buy the item.

COMMUNICATION
Talking about transportation ▪ Describing feelings ▪ Identifying people by physical appearance

GRAMMAR
Prepositions: *from* (place) *to* (place); *by* + vehicle ▪ *Be* and *feel* + adjective ▪ Prepositions: *before* and *after* ▪ Question: Which one?

# At the Airport

*The Navas are at the airport. Their flight to Los Angeles leaves in half an hour. They're all happy and excited about their trip to the United States.*

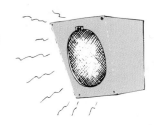

World Airlines Flight 987 to Los Angeles is now ready for boarding. Passengers holding tickets please proceed to Gate 3.

ANA:        Oh, Mom, I'm so excited.
MELANIE:    You know, I am too.

PABLO:      Where's Carlos?
ANA:        He went to get something to read. There he is. Over there at the newsstand next to the tall man.
MELANIE:    Which one?
ANA:        The one with the red hair.

WOMAN:      It's a beautiful day for flying, isn't it?
MELANIE:    Yes, it is. Are you going to Los Angeles?
WOMAN:      No. San Francisco. And you?
MELANIE:    L.A. My parents live there, so it's always our first stop.
WOMAN:      And where else are you going?
MELANIE:    The Grand Canyon, Santa Fe, Washington, D.C., and New York.
WOMAN:      Are you flying everywhere?
MELANIE:    We're driving from L.A. to the Grand Canyon and Santa Fe. Then we're flying to Washington and taking the train to New York.
WOMAN:      What a wonderful trip!

# 1 Presentation

## Talking about transportation

1. The Navas are flying **from** Mexico City **to** Los Angeles.
2. They are going from Mexico City to Los Angeles **by plane.**
3. They are driving **from** Los Angeles **to** the Grand Canyon.
4. They are going from Los Angeles to the Grand Canyon **by car.**

A
A: The Navas are going from Mexico City to L.A.
B: How are they traveling?
A: | By plane.
| They're flying.

B
A: How do you get to school?
B: I walk. It takes me ten minutes.

**Useful vocabulary:**

fly = go by plane

drive = go by car

take a | taxi | = go by | taxi |
| cab | | cab |

take a train = go by train

go by boat

go by bus

go on my bike

walk

# 2 Practice

**Work with a partner. Make sentences about where the people are going and how they got there. Use conversation model A in *1*.**

1. Toshio / New York – Winfield // cab
2. Navas / Winfield – New York City // train
3. Gloria's mother / San Juan - St. Thomas // boat
4. Gino / New York - Chicago // plane
5. The Logans / Winfield - New York City // bus
6. Cristina / New York - Washington // plane
7. The Youngs / Winfield - Boston // car
8. Liz / New York City - Winfield // bus
9. Kanskys / Los Angeles - Hawaii // boat
10. Gloria / Washington - New York // train

## 3 Interaction

**Talk with a partner about how you get to different places.**

> A: How do you get to _____ ?
> B: _____ . It takes me _____ . How about you?
> A: _____ . It takes me _____ .

## 4 Vocabulary in Context

### Describing feelings

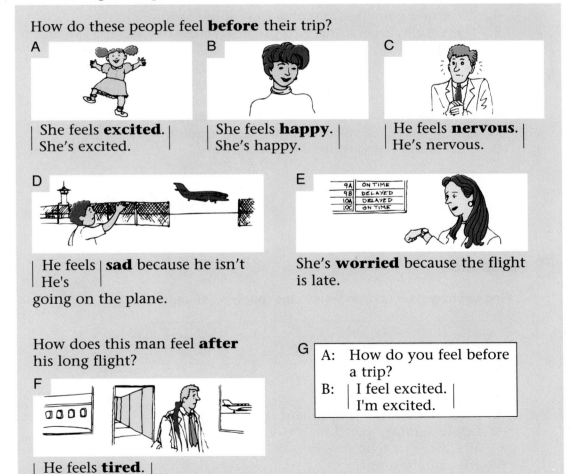

How do these people feel **before** their trip?

A
She feels **excited**.
She's excited.

B
She feels **happy**.
She's happy.

C
He feels **nervous**.
He's nervous.

D
He feels | **sad** because he isn't
He's |
going on the plane.

E
She's **worried** because the flight is late.

How does this man feel **after** his long flight?

F
He feels **tired**.
He's tired.

G
A: How do you feel before a trip?
B: | I feel excited. |
| I'm excited. |

## 5 Practice

**Talk about how the following people feel.**

> Bob has a big geometry exam tomorrow. He doesn't understand everything.
> A: He's worried.
> B: Maybe he feels nervous.
> C: He isn't happy.

1. Gino is finishing a hard day at work.
2. Lisa has to go to the doctor.
3. Tomorrow is Joyce's birthday.
4. Cristina is going to Colombia to visit her family.
5. The Youngs are waiting for Mike and Ted. Mike has the car, and they are late.
6. Adela has a computer exam tomorrow. She doesn't understand everything.
7. Mike and Bob have an important soccer game tomorrow.
8. Sam's car was in the parking lot. Now he can't find it.
9. Toshio is in Caracas. He doesn't have friends there.
10. Liz is going out with her boyfriend, Dave.

## 6 Interaction

**Find out how your partner feels in the following situations:**

> A: How do you feel _____ ?
> B: I _____ .

1. before an exam
2. before a trip
3. before a dentist appointment
4. before summer vacation
5. after work or school
6. after a hard exam
7. after an easy exam
8. after summer vacation

### Identifying people by physical appearance

*By height*

A

1. He's short.
   The short one.
2. He's tall.
   The tall one.

*By use of glasses*

B

1. The man with the glasses.
2. The one without glasses.

*By hair color and length*

C

1. The boy with long, blond hair.
2. The boy with long, brown hair.
3. The boy with short, black hair.
4. The boy with short, red hair.

*By clothing*

D

1. The tall girl in the red dress.
2. The tall girl in the green skirt.
3. The tall girl in the pink blouse.

E
> A: Where's Carlos?
> B: Over there next to the tall man.
> A: Which one?
> B: The one with the glasses.

F
> A: I'd like to meet that man.
> B: Which one?
> A: The short one.

**Pronunciation**

**Repeat these phrases.**

1. the man

   the short man

   the short man with black hair

2. the girl

   the short girl

   the short girl in the green skirt

3. the boy

   the tall boy

   the tall boy with the long, brown hair

4. the woman

   the tall woman

   the tall woman with the glasses

9 **Practice**

**Practice with a partner. Take turns asking where Carlos is. Use conversation model E in 7.**

1. tall girl / glasses
2. short boy / blue shirt
3. tall woman / blond hair
4. short man / pink shirt
5. tall boy / red hair

6. short boy / short, brown hair
7. short girl / glasses
8. tall man / long, black hair
9. short woman / short, red hair
10. tall man / brown pants

10 **Listening**

**Number your paper from 1-8. Listen to the descriptions and write the letter of the person.**

> YOU HEAR: I'd like to meet the girl with the blond hair.
> WRITE: ___A___

A

B

C

D

## 11 Reading

### Before You Read

Ana Nava lives in Mexico City. Her full name is Ana Kansky Nava. Her address is Calle Paloma, 5. Ana writes Mexico, D.F., for Mexico City when she fills out a card like this. She was born on September 4, 1976, in Mexico City, Mexico. She is a citizen of Mexico. She has a passport with a visa because she is traveling to a foreign country. She went to the U.S. Embassy in Mexico City to get her visa on November 11, 1989. Her passport number is M734056.

Ana and her family are on World Airlines Flight 987. In Los Angeles, they are staying with her grandparents, Julia and Joseph Kansky at 463 Lake Road in Los Angeles, California.

Before she can enter the United States, Ana has to fill out an entry card. Look at the blank card. Talk about the information she needs to write on the card.

> Ana has to write her name.

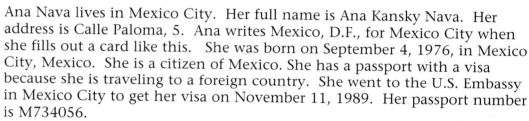

| | |
|---|---|
| **PLEASE TYPE OR PRINT CLEARLY PRESS FIRMLY BOTH COPIES MUST BE LEGIBLE** | Family Name *(Capital Letters)*    First Name    Middle Initial |
| | 1                        2              3 |
| *(DO NOT USE PENCIL)* | Country of Citizenship    Passport or Alien Registration Number    Permit Number    **866 47 15** |
| | 4                        5 |
| All passengers, except U.S. Citizens, complete this form. Immigrants and Permanent Resident Aliens complete top four lines only. | * United States Address *(Number, Street, City and State)* |
| | 6 |
| | ** Airline and Flight No. or Vessel of Arrival    ** Passenger Boarded at |
| | 7                        8 |
| * Foreign Visitors: Give Address Where You Can be Located. | Number, Street, City, Province *(State)* and Country of Permanent Residence |
| | 9 |
| | Month, Day and Year of Birth |
| | 10 |
| ** To be completed Only For Arrival in U.S. | City, Province *(State)* and Country of Birth |
| | 11 |
| **THIS FORM REQUIRED BY U.S. IMMIGRATION & NATURALIZATION SERVICE.** | Visa Issued at *(If no visa, insert ticket number)* |
| | 12 |
| *(DO NOT FOLD)* | **STAPLE HERE**    Month, Day and Year Visa Issued |
| | 13 |

A NONIMMIGRANT ALIEN WHO ACCEPTS UNAUTHORIZED EMPLOYMENT IS SUBJECT TO DEPORTATION

Surrender this copy When Leaving The United States SEE REVERSE

FORM 1-94

## 12 Writing

Number your paper from 1-12. Find the information Ana needs to fill out her entry card. Write the information on your paper.

## 13 Final Activity

A. What famous people do you know well? Can you bring pictures of them to class? Put the pictures where everyone can see them. Choose three pictures. Write one or two sentences to describe each person.

> He is a tall man with short, black hair.
> He is wearing glasses.

B. Read one of your descriptions out loud. Can your classmates match your description with the correct picture?

**COMMUNICATION**
Talking about a trip ▪ Talking about quantity

**GRAMMAR**
Past tense: *drive, fly, take* ▪ Preposition: *for* with days, months, and years ▪ Quantifier: *a lot of* + noun

## In New York

*The Navas are in Winfield. They're staying at the Plaza Hotel. They have a beautiful view of Winfield Bay. Yesterday they went into New York City with Mike, Ted, and Joyce Young. In the morning they went to the Museum of Modern Art. They saw a lot of beautiful paintings. After lunch they went to Yankee Stadium for the baseball game.*

*This morning they took the train back to New York City. Then they took the subway to Chinatown. They had lunch at a Chinese restaurant. Then they took a cab to the World Trade Center. They are on the 107th floor of the World Trade Center now.*

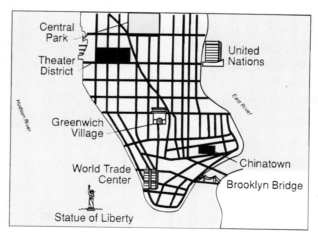

CARLOS: Wow! This is incredible!
MELANIE: Look over there, Ana. There's the Statue of Liberty.
ANA: It's beautiful, isn't it?
PABLO: Come over here. There's the Brooklyn Bridge.
ANA: Are you taking pictures of all this, Dad?
PABLO: No, we can buy better pictures at the gift shop.
ANA: OK. Maybe I can find something for Grandma Maria at the gift shop, too.

**Unit Eighteen**     167

## 1 Presentation

### Talking about the past

| Use **for** + | days<br>months<br>years | to say how long. |
|---|---|---|

| Present | Past |
|---|---|
| fly | flew |
| drive | drove |
| take | took |

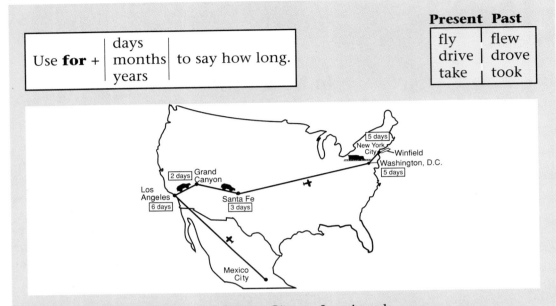

1. The Navas **flew** from Mexico City to Los Angeles.
   They were in L.A. **for** six days.
2. They **drove** from L.A. to the Grand Canyon.
   They were at the Grand Canyon **for** two days.
3. They **took** the train from Washington to New York.
   They are in New York now.

## 2 Practice

Tell about the Navas' trip, following the route on the map.

## 3 Reentry

Ask and answer questions about how many days the Navas were in Los Angeles, at the Grand Canyon, in Santa Fe, and in Washington.

A:  Were the Navas in Los Angeles for three days?
B:  No, they weren't.  They were there for six days.

## 4

**Listening**

Number your paper from 1-10. Look at the map in *1* that shows the route the Navas took. Listen to the sentences and write *yes* or *no*.

> You hear: The Navas went to San Francisco.
> Write: ___no___

---

**5** **Reentry**

| Prepositions | Time Expressions | Place Expressions |
|---|---|---|
| **in** | in \| July \|<br>\| 1990 \|<br>in the \| morning \|<br>\| afternoon \|<br>\| evening \|<br>\| spring \| | in Boston<br>in Massachusetts<br>in the United States |
| **on** | on Friday<br>on the weekend | on Kennedy Avenue |
| **at** | at 10:30 am<br>at night | at the hotel<br>at \| home \|<br>\| school \|<br>\| work \|<br>at 426 Kennedy Avenue |

Complete the sentences with the correct preposition.

1. Bob is _____ home right now.
   He's leaving for school _____ ten minutes.
2. Ana's grandparents live _____ 463 Lake Road _____ Los Angeles, California. The Navas are leaving for L.A. _____ Wednesday.
3. Lisa is _____ the library. The library is _____ Ocean Avenue. She's going home _____ 4:30.
4. It's usually hot _____ New York _____ the summer.
5. I like to study _____ the morning.
6. I clean the house _____ Saturday morning.
7. Nhu Trinh was born _____ Vietnam _____ 1968.
8. Melanie was born _____ May.
9. Elinor works _____ Winfield Hospital. She rarely works _____ night.
10. I leave for work _____ 6:00 _____ the morning.

## 6 Pronunciation

**Repeat these sentences.**

1. I'm going tomorrow.

   I'm going tomorrow at ten thirty.

   I'm going tomorrow at ten thirty in the morning.

2. The Kanskys live in Los Angeles.

   They live on Lake Road in Los Angeles.

   They live at four-sixty-three Lake Road in Los Angeles.

## 7 Presentation

**Talking about quantity**

1. The Navas went to the Museum of Modern Art.
   They saw **a lot of** beautiful paintings.
2. They went to the International Supermarket.
   They saw **a lot of** beautiful fresh fruit.

## 8 Practice

**Talk about what the Navas saw in each place. Use the cues and your imagination. Ask your teacher for vocabulary you need.**

> Chinatown / people
> The Navas went to Chinatown.
> They saw a lot of people.
> They saw a lot of Chinese restaurants.

1. the World Trade Center / tall buildings
2. The International Supermarket / vegetables
3. Yankee Stadium / people
4. Winfield / friends
5. Washington, D.C. / beautiful buildings
6. Santa Fe / Spanish churches

## 9 Practice

**Tell about a place you went to recently and what you saw there.**

I went to _____the supermarket_____ . I saw _____my friend Marta_____ .
I saw _____a lot of food_____ . I saw _____some beautiful apples_____ .

I went to _____Warner's Department Store_____ .
I saw _____a lot of jeans on sale_____ .
I saw _____some beautiful shirts_____ .

## 10 Vocabulary in Context

### Souvenirs

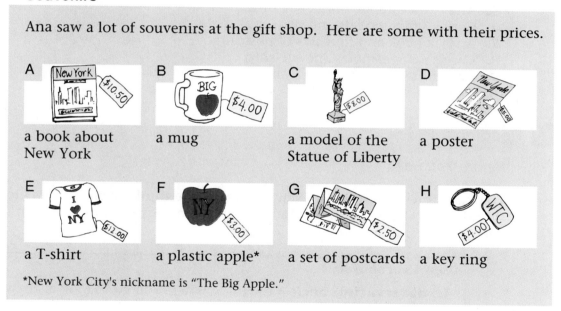

Ana saw a lot of souvenirs at the gift shop. Here are some with their prices.

A — a book about New York $10.50

B — a mug $4.00

C — a model of the Statue of Liberty $8.00

D — a poster $5.00

E — a T-shirt $12.00

F — a plastic apple* $3.00

G — a set of postcards $2.50

H — a key ring $4.00

*New York City's nickname is "The Big Apple."

## 11 Practice

**Take turns asking and answering questions about the price of the different souvenirs.**

A: How much does the book about New York cost?
B: It costs $10.50.

## 12 Reentry

**Talking about cost**

**Work with a partner. Take turns asking questions and calculating the answers.
Ana has $20. Carlos has $30.**

> Carlos / two T-shirts
> A:    Can Carlos buy two T-shirts?
> B:    Yes, he can.  They cost $24.  He has $30.

1. Ana / two books about New York
2. Carlos / two mugs and a T-shirt
3. Carlos / three models of the Statue of Liberty
4. Ana / two posters and three mugs
5. Ana / three apples and a key ring
6. Carlos / two models and two T-shirts
7. Ana / a book and four sets of postcards
8. Carlos / three apples and a T-shirt
9. Carlos / two books and a T-shirt
10. Ana / six sets of postcards

## 13 Reading

### Before You Read

You have three free hours in New York.  You are thinking about going to the
World Trade Center.  You have a brochure.  What kinds of information do
you need to find out from the brochure?

> **Useful vocabulary:**
> 1. **observation deck** = the place where you go to look at the view
>
> 2. second **floor**
>    first **floor**
>    basement
> 3. **all directions** = north, south, east, west
> 4. **snack bar** = place where you can eat snacks (small meals)
> 5. **concourse** = a large, open place where you can walk
> 6. **coins:** Nickels, dimes, and quarters are American coins.
> 7. **free:** If something is free, you don't have to pay money for it.
> 8. **fast food restaurant:** You order and they serve the food fast.

## THE OBSERVATION DECK

On the 107th floor of the World Trade Center, you feel like you are in heaven. You can see the horizon in all directions - the Statue of Liberty, New Jersey, the Hudson River, the George Washington Bridge, the skyscrapers of midtown Manhattan, the East River, the Brooklyn Bridge and boats in the busy harbor. At the top, you can eat at a snack bar and shop for a souvenir at the gift shop. The Observation Deck is open from 9:30 AM to 9:30 PM every day; for more information call (212) 466-7377.

## SHOPPING AND RESTAURANTS

On the Concourse you can shop at dozens of stores and buy everything from clothes to gold coins. Parking is free in the basement garage on Saturday from 10:00 AM to 6:00 PM with a $5.00 purchase in any Concourse store or restaurant. Restaurants at the World Trade Center serve everything from hot dogs to steak and from soup to dessert. Two of the many possibilities are:

## WINDOWS ON THE WORLD

(212) 938-1111. (Jackets and ties required for gentlemen. No jeans please.) 107th floor of One World Trade Center. The menu offers food from all over the world including typical American Cuisine. Open from 3:00 PM-1:00 AM, Monday - Friday; 12:00 PM-1:00 AM , Saturday; and 12:00 PM - midnight, Sunday.

## THE BIG KITCHEN

(212) 938-1153. Eight fast food restaurants in one. Open 7:00 AM-7:00 PM, Monday - Friday and 10:00 AM -5:00 PM, on Saturday.

## After You Read

**A. Answer these questions about the Observation Deck. Say *Yes, No,* or *I don't know.***

1. Can you see south from the Observation Deck?
2. Can you get something to eat on the Observation Deck?
3. Can you buy a gift on the Observation Deck?
4. Can you go up to the Observation Deck at 10:00 pm?
5. Does it cost money to visit the Observation Deck?

**B. Now answer these questions about shopping and restaurants.**

1. What can you buy in the stores on the Concourse?
2. When is parking free?
3. What kind of clothes should you wear to **Windows on the World?**
4. When can you eat at **Windows on the World** during the week?
5. What kind of restaurants are in **The Big Kitchen?** When can you eat there?

## 14 Writing

Here is a postcard Ana wrote to her grandparents in California. Imagine you are on a trip. Write a postcard to a friend. Use Ana's postcard as your model.

Dear Grandma & Grandpa,
    I love NY! We're having a great time. Today we went to the top of the World Trade Center. It was a beautiful day, and we saw everything! We had a great time with you, too. Thank you for everything.
                        Love, Ana

July 27

Mr. & Mrs. Joseph Kansky
463 Lake Road
Los Angeles, California
            90052

## 15 Final Activity

Tell about a short or a long trip. Tell where you went, how you got there, how many hours, days, or weeks you were there, and what you saw.

I went to Allen's Department Store last Saturday. I was there for an hour. I saw a lot of nice clothes . I saw my friend Mary.

I went to Chicago last year. I went by plane. I was in Chicago for one week. I saw my sister and her husband. I went to a baseball game. I had a great time.

# Appendix A

## Countries, Nationalities, and Languages

| Country | Nationality | Language(s) |
|---|---|---|
| Algeria | Algerian | Arabic/Berber |
| Argentina | Argentinian | Spanish |
| Australia | Australian | English |
| Bolivia | Bolivian | Spanish |
| Brazil | Brazilian | Portuguese |
| Cambodia | Cambodian | Khmer |
| Canada | Canadian | English/French |
| Chile | Chilean | Spanish |
| China | Chinese | Chinese |
| Colombia | Colombian | Spanish |
| Costa Rica | Costa Rican | Spanish |
| Cuba | Cuban | Spanish |
| Czechoslovakia | Czech | Czech/Slovak |
| Denmark | Danish | Danish |
| the Dominican Republic | Dominican | Spanish |
| Ecuador | Ecuadorean | Spanish |
| Egypt | Egyptian | Arabic |
| El Salvador | Salvadorean | Spanish |
| England | English | English |
| Ethiopia | Ethiopian | Amharic |
| France | French | French |
| Germany | German | German |
| Great Britain | British | English |
| Greece | Greek | Greek |
| Guatemala | Guatemalan | Spanish |
| Haiti | Haitian | French |
| Honduras | Honduran | Spanish |
| India | Indian | Hindi/English |
| Indonesia | Indonesian | Bahasa Indonesia |
| Iraq | Iraqi | Arabic |
| Israel | Israeli | Hebrew/Arabic |
| Italy | Italian | Italian |
| Japan | Japanese | Japanese |
| Jordan | Jordanian | Arabic |
| Kenya | Kenyan | Swahili |
| Korea | Korean | Korean |
| Laos | Laotian | Lao |
| Lebanon | Lebanese | Arabic |
| Mexico | Mexican | Spanish |
| Nicaragua | Nicaraguan | Spanish |
| Nigeria | Nigerian | English/Hausa/Ibo/Yoruba |
| Norway | Norwegian | Norwegian |
| Pakistan | Pakistani | Urdu/Punjabi/English |
| Panama | Panamanian | Spanish |

| | | |
|---|---|---|
| Paraguay | Paraguayan | Spanish |
| Peru | Peruvian | Spanish |
| the Philippines | Filipino | Pilipino/English/Spanish |
| Poland | Polish | Polish |
| Portugal | Portuguese | Portuguese |
| Puerto Rico | Puerto Rican | Spanish |
| Saudia Arabia | Saudi Arabian | Arabic |
| the Soviet Union | Soviet/Russian | Russian |
| Spain | Spanish | Spanish |
| Sweden | Swedish | Swedish |
| Syria | Syrian | Syrian |
| Tanzania | Tanzanian | Swahili/English |
| Thailand | Thai | Thai |
| Turkey | Turkish | Turkish |
| the United States | American | English |
| Uruguay | Uruguayan | Spanish |
| Venezuela | Venezuelan | Spanish |
| Zaire | Zairian | French/Bantu |

## Appendix B

### Occupations

accountant
actor
actress
architect
artist
athlete
baker
bank teller
barber
bookkeeper
bus driver
butcher
carpenter
cashier
clerk
computer operator
computer programmer
construction worker
cook
counselor
dancer
dental hygienist
dentist
doctor
editor
electrician
engineer

factory worker
farmer
fashion designer
file clerk
firefighter
flight attendant
hairdresser
homemaker
housekeeper
insurance agent
jeweler
lawyer
letter carrier
librarian
machine operator
maintenance worker
mason
mechanic
model
musician
newscaster
nurse
painter
pharmacist
physical therapist
pilot
plumber

police officer
postal clerk
professor
psychologist
receptionist
reporter
salesperson
scientist
secretary
security guard
shipping clerk
singer
social worker
tailor
taxi driver
teacher
telephone operator
travel agent
truck driver
typist
veterinarian
waiter
waitress
writer

# Appendix C

## Irregular Verbs

| | | | |
|---|---|---|---|
| be | was/were | meet | met* |
| come | came | put | put |
| cost | cost | read | read |
| do | did | ride | rode |
| drink | drank | say | said |
| drive | drove* | see | saw* |
| eat | ate | sing | sang |
| feel | felt | sleep | slept |
| fly | flew* | speak | spoke |
| get | got | swim | swam |
| go | went* | take | took* |
| have | had* | wear | wore |
| hurt | hurt | write | wrote |
| lie down | lay down | | |

* Past tense form taught in Book 1.

# Appendix D

## Phonetic Symbols

### Consonants

| | |
|---|---|
| [p] | piano, apple |
| [t] | ten, can't |
| [k] | coffee, like |
| [b] | bank, cabbage |
| [d] | dinner, idea |
| [g] | good, drugstore |
| [f] | five, after |
| [v] | very, have |
| [θ] | thirsty, with |
| [ð] | the, mother |
| [s] | some, dress |
| [z] | zero, busy |
| [š] | shoe, information |
| [ž] | pleasure, measure |
| [č] | children, teach |
| [ǰ] | juice, age |
| [l] | letter, mile |
| [r] | right, sorry |
| [m] | many, name |
| [n] | never, money |
| [ŋ] | key ring, sing |
| [w] | water, housework |
| [y] | year, million |

### Vowels

| | |
|---|---|
| [iy] | meet, tea |
| [i] | in, city |
| [ey] | waiter, great |
| [e] | hello, help |
| [æ] | ask, family |
| [ə] | appointment, but |
| [a] | father, hot |
| [uw] | you, room |
| [u] | could, put |
| [ow] | home, go |
| [ɔ] | water, long |
| [ay] | dime, night |
| [aw] | pound, house |
| [ɔy] | boy, join |

# VOCABULARY

The vocabulary list contains the productive words as well as the receptive words in the textbook. Productive words are those that students should know how to use. The unit number refers to when the word is first introduced productively. Receptive words are those that students need only understand. The unit number for these words is in parentheses.

*(n)* = noun; *(v)* = verb; *(adj)* = adjective

**A**

a   1
ability   (5)
about   11
ache   12
across from   7
activity   (4)
actor   1
actress   1
ad   (7)
add   9
address   3
adult   (12)
advertisement   (7)
advice   (12)
after   17
afternoon   1
aged   (11)
agency   11
airplane   (5)
airport   (6)
aisle   7
algebra   16
a little   5
all   (3), 7
all over   (12)
almost never   13
a lot of   (6), 1, 5
alphabet   (2)
also   7
altitude   (13)
always   13
am   1
American   5
an   1
and   2
announcer   (8)
another   6
answer   3
any   15
anything   7
apartment   11

apple   7
appointment   5
April   3
architect   (13)
are   1
arrive   (15)
artist   1
ask for   2
aspirin   12
at   3
athletic   (5)
Atlantic   (13)
at night   8
August   3
autumn   13
avenue (ave.)   3
awful   8


**B**

babysit   4
back *(n)*   12
backache   12
bacon   (10)
bad   (13)
bag   7
baked potato   (10)
banana   7
bank   6
baseball   12
basement   (18)
basil   (9)
basketball   3
basketball court   4
bathroom   3
bay   (6)
be   1
be back   (9)
be born   (5), 14
be broke   (10)
be careful   (12)
be late   (13)

be like   6
beach   (2), 12
beans   7
beautiful   (4), 8
because   13
bedroom   3
beef   7
before   17
beige   16
best in town   (10)
better   12
beverage   (10)
bicycle (bike)   3
big   6
biology   16
birth certificate   (3)
birthday   (16), 17
black   16
blond   17
blouse   16
blue   16
board   3
boarding   (17)
boat   17
bone   (7)
boneless   (7)
book   1, 4
bookstore   6
born   1, 4
both   (14)
bottle   7
boulevard (blvd.)   3
box   7
boy   (11), 16
boy *(exclamation)*   10
boyfriend   2
Brazil   5
Brazilian   5
bread   7
breakfast 9
bridge   (18)
bring   (14)

brother   2
brown   16
brownies   (9)
buck   (10)
building   (13)
bun   (10)
bus   (14), 17
business   (8)
bus station   6
busy   4
but   5
butter   7
buy   7
by   17
bye   1

## C

cab   17
cabbage   7
cafeteria   (5)
cake   7
call *(v)*   3
can/can't   5
can *(n)*   7
candy   6
candy store   6
canned   7
cantaloupe   (7)
capital *(adj)*   2
capital *(n)*   (13)
caption   (5)
car   3
card   (17)
carrot   (7)
cart   (7)
cartoon   (8)
cashier   1
cat   3
caution   (12)
Celsius   (13)
cent   10
center   (18)
cereal   7
channel   8
checkout   (7)
cheese   7
cheeseburger   (10)
chemistry   16
chicken   7

child/children   2
China   5
Chinese   (2), 5
choice   (7)
chopped (nuts)   (9)
church   6
cinema   (8)
citizenship   (17)
city   3
city hall   6
clarinet   5
class   5
clean   4
cleaning products   (7)
clerk   16
climate   (13)
close *(v)*   1
closet   3
clothes   (18)
clothing   (17)
c'mon   (4)
coast   (13)
cocoa   (9)
coffee   7
coin   18
cola   10
cold *(adj)*   13
cold *(n)*   12
cold medicine   12
cole slaw   (10)
coliseum   (6)
Colombia   5
Colombian   5
color   16
combination   10
combine   (9)
come   3
come along   6
come from   (8)
commercial   8
common   (9)
community college   6
complete   (13)
computer programming
   (7), 11
concert   8
concourse   (18)
congratulations   16
cook   1
cooking *(n)*   8

cool *(v)*   (9)
cool *(adj)*   13
copy   (9)
corn   7
corned beef   (10)
cost   10
cough   12
cough drops   12
country   5
couple of bucks   (10)
court   4
cousin   (5)
cuisine   (18)
cup   (9), 10
customer   16

## D

dad   3
dairy product   (7)
dance   5
date   5
date filed   (3)
date issued   (3)
date of birth   14
daughter   2
day   (6), 8
day off   8
dead   15
dear *(salutation)*   (14)
deceased   15
December   3
deck   (18)
delicious   9
dentist   12
dessert   (18)
difficult   (13)
dime   10
dining room   3
dinner   9
direction   (18)
dish *(food)*   (9)
dishes   11
district   (18)
divorced   15
dizzy   12
do   1; don't   8
doctor   1
does/doesn't   8
dog   3

dollar   10
dozen   7
draw   5
dress   16
drew   (13)
drink   10
drive   5
drove   18
drug   6
drugstore   6
drums   5
dry   9
duchess   (5)
dumb   8
during   8

**E**

ear   12
earache   12
east   3
easy   16
eat   9
egg   7
eight   1
eighteen   1
eighteenth   5
eighth   5
eighty   2
electrician   1
eleven   1
eleventh   5
else   7
embassy   (17)
end   (16)
engineer   1
engineering   8
English   5
enter   (17)
evening   1
every   8
everyone   (8)
everything   (2), 10
everywhere   (17)
exam   5
excellent   8
excited   17
excuse me   2
extra large   16

**F**

Fahrenheit   (13)
fall *(n)*   13
family   2
famous   (5)
farewell   (1)
fast   5
fast food   (18)
father   2
favor   7
favorite   (7), 9
February   3
feel   12
feel (well)   12
feet   (13)
fever   12
fifteen   1
fifteenth   5
fifth   5
fifty   2
fill out   (17)
find   (6)
fine   1
finish   15
fire station   6
first   5
first name   3
five   1
fix   4
flew   18
flight   (13), 17
floor   (18)
floor plan   7
flour   7
flu   12
fly   (5), 17
food   7
football   5
for   9
for + *(time)*   9
foreign   (17)
form   3
forty   2
four   1
fourteen   1
fourteenth   5
fourth   5
France   5
free   (18)
French   5

french fries   (10)
fresh   (7), 9
Friday   3
friend   2
friendly   (5)
from   5
from *(time)* to *(time)*   8
front   (12)
frozen   9
frozen food   7
fruit   7
full name   3
fun   (11)

**G**

gallon (gal)   7
game   (5), 8
garage   3
garden center   (7)
garlic   (9)
gate   (17)
gave   (5)
gentlemen   (18)
geometry   16
get   10
get a (cold, flu)   12
get a gift   (16)
get going   (14)
get some rest   12
gift shop   18
gift wrapped   (16)
girl   (11), 16
girlfriend   2
give   1
glass   10
glasses   17
go   4; goes   8
go out   11
gold   (18)
good   9
good afternoon   1
good-bye   1
good evening   1
good morning   1
good night   1
grandchildren   15
granddaughter   15
grandfather   15
grandmother   15

grandparents 15
grandson 15
grape 7
graph (11)
gray 16
greased (pan) (9)
great 1
green 16
greeting (1)
group 3
guitar 5


**H**

hair 17
half gallon 7
ham (10)
hamburger (10)
happy (13), 17
harbor (18)
hard (13), 16
has 8
has to 15
hate 13
have 8
have to 4
Hawaii (13)
he 1
he's 1
head 12
headache 12
head of lettuce 9
health professional (12)
heaven (18)
height (17)
helicopter (5)
hello 1
help (5), 11
her 2
here 6
here's 6
here comes (2)
hey 5
hi 1
his 2
history 16
home 3
homemaker 1
homework (11)
hon (7)

honey 12
Hong Kong (13)
hope (v) 12
hope so 16
horizon (18)
horse (5)
hospital 3
hot 13
hot chocolate (10)
hot dog 7
hotel 6
hour (8), 9
house (4)
housework 11
how 1
how's 1
how about 7
how are you 1
how many 9
how much 9
how much (cost) 10
how old 11
how's everything 1
how's it going (7)
hundred 2
hungry 10
hurt 12
husband 2


**I**

I 1
I'll 3
I'm 1
ice cream 7
iced (coffee/tea) (10)
ice skate 13
idea 4
identification (17)
identifying 2
if 2
if not (15)
immigration official (14)
in 3
in fact (14)
including (18)
incredible (18)
information (3)
ingredients (9)
instrument (5)

interesting 8
interior (13)
international (17)
interviewer (13)
into 9
introduce (13)
is 1
isn't 1
it 1
it's 1
it sure does (8)
Italian 5
Italy 5
item (7)


**J**

jacket (18)
January 3
Japan 5
Japanese 5
jeans 16
job (10)
juice 7
July 3
jumbo (10)
June 3
just 3


**K**

ketchup 7
key ring 18
kids 2
kilometer (13)
kind (n) (9)
kitchen 3
Korea 5
Korean 5


**L**

ladies and gentlemen (9)
language 5
large (7), 9
largest (13)
last month 13
last name 3
last night 13

last week   13
last year   13
late   (8)
later   1
laundry   11
leave for   (14)
lemon   12
lemonade   (10)
length   (17)
let's   4
letter   (5)
lettuce   7
librarian   (8)
library   6
lie down   12
like + *(n)*   8
like to + *(v)*   10, 13
liquid   12
listed   (7)
listen to   1
little   16
live *(v)*   8
living room   3
loaf/loaves   7
located   (13)
location   (6)
long   17
look + *(adj)*   9
look at   1
look for   16
look like   (6)
look up   (5)
love   13
lunch   9

M

ma'am   7
major (13)
make   8
man/men   16
manage   (11)
manager   (7)
many   (9)
map   (6)
March   3
margarine   7
marina   6
married   2
marvelous   8

master *(adj)*   (13)
math   (10)
May   3
may I help you   (7), 16
maybe   (10), 12
mayonnaise   (7)
me   7
me too   10
meal   (18)
mean   6
measurement   (9)
meat   7
mechanic   1
medium   10
meet   1
melon   (7)
melted   (9)
menu   (10)
met   14
meter   (13)
Mexican   5
Mexico   5
middle initial   3
middle name   3
midnight   (18)
midtown   (18)
mile   (13)
milk   7
minute   3
mix   (9)
model   18
modern   (13)
Mom   (3)
Monday   3
month   (3), 15
more   (18)
morning   1
most   (11)
mother   2
move   3
movies   4
Mr.   1
Mrs.   1
Ms.   1
mug   18
museum   6
mushroom   9
music   4
mustard   (7)
my   1

my place   (4)

N

name   1
nasal spray   12
nation   (18)
nationality   5
navy   (5)
near   6
need   7
nervous   17
never   13
news   8
newspaper   4
newsstand   (17)
next month   15
next summer   15
next to   (5), 7
next week   15
next year   15
nice   8
nice to meet you   1
nickel   10
nickname   3
night   1
nine   1
nineteen   1
nineteenth   5
ninety   2
ninth   5
no   1
noon   1
north   3
nose   12
not   3
not bad   16
not exactly   (5)
not too good   12
note   (4)
nothing much   15
November   3
now   10
number   3
nurse   1
nursing a baby   (12)
nuts   (9)

## O

o'clock   4
oatmeal   7
observation deck   (18)
October   3
of   7
offer   (18)
office   3
oh   2
oh no   5
oil   7
OK   1
old   (6), 9
older   (12)
on   6
on sale   (7)
one   1
one (pronoun)   17
onion   7
only   10
open   1
optional   (9)
or   11
orange (n)   7, (adj)   16
order   10
oregano   (9)
originally   5
other   (5), 12
ounce (oz)   7
our   2
out loud   3
outside   (11)
over there   7

## P

package   7
pain   (12)
pain relief   (12)
paint   4
painting (n)   (18)
pair   16
pan   9
pants   16
paper   1
paper goods   (7)
parents   2
park (n)   4
parking lot   3

partner   3
part-time   (10)
pass (an exam)   16
passenger   (13)
passport   (17)
pastrami   (10)
pear   7
peas   7
pen   6
penny   10
people   2
pepper   7
pepperoni   10
permit   (17)
person   2
pharmacist   (12)
phone   3
physician   (12)
physics   16
piano   5
pick up   12
pickle   (10)
picture   (1)
piece of paper   1
pilot   (5)
pinch of   (9)
pink   16
pint   7
pizza   10
place   (4)
plain   10
plan   (13)
plane   (5), 17
plastic   18
plate (dish)   (10)
play (v)   4
please   3
plenty of   12
point   3
police officer   1
police station   6
pool   4
Portuguese   5
possibility   (18)
postcard   18
poster   18
post office   6
potato   7
potato chips   7
pound (lb)   7

pour   9
powder   (9)
pregnant   (12)
pretty (adj)   (6)
price   10
prince   (5)
print   (3)
problem   (4)
program   8
programming   (7)
pronounce   6
purchase   (18)
pure (beef)   (10)
purple   16
put   9
put away   1

## Q

quart (qt)   7
quarter   10
queen   (5)
question   3

## R

racquet   (4)
rain (v)   (13)
rarely   13
read   3
ready   (13)
really + (adj)   (8)
recipe   8
red   16
regards to   (14)
registration card   (3)
relax   4
required   (18)
rest   12
restaurant   1
restaurant cashier   1
rice   7
ride   5
right   3
right away   12
right here   6
right now   (7)
river   (18)
road (rd.)   3
rock (music)   (8)

rock concert   12
roller skate   5
room   3
run   5
Russian   5

S

sad   17
salad   9
salt   7
same   (11)
sandals   16
sandwich   (10)
Saturday   3
sausage   7
sauce   8
saw (v)   14
say   1
schedule   (8)
school   3
season (n)   13
season (v)   9
second   5
see   1
see you then   12
seek   (12)
sentence   3
September   3
set   18
seven   1
seventeen   1
seventeenth   5
seventh   5
seventy   2
share   11
she   1
she's   1
shirt   16
shoes   16
shop   (18)
shopper   (7)
shopping   (18)
shopping list   (9)
short   3
shorts   16
should   12
sick   14
side order   (10)
sing   5

single   15
sir   10
sirloin   (7)
sister   2
sit   3
sit down   3
site   (13)
six   1
sixteen   1
sixteenth   5
sixth   5
sixty   2
size   16
skate   13
ski   5
skinny   17
skirt   16
skyscraper   (18)
slacks   16
sleep   4
slice (v)   9
slice (n)   10
sliced (eggs)   (10)
slicing (tomatoes)   (7)
small   6
smart   (8)
smell   9
snack bar   (18)
snack foods   (7)
sneakers   16
so + (adj)   (15)
soccer   5
socks   16
soda   10
soft drinks   7
some   7
something   10
sometimes   13
son   2
soon   12
sore throat   12
sorry   4
sound good   10
soup   7
south   3
South America   13
souvenir   18
Soviet Union   5
spaghetti   7
Spanish   5

speak   5
speaking   (7)
split   (10)
sponsor   (8)
sports   8
sports events   (6)
spring   13
square (adj)   (9)
stadium   (6)
stand up   3
state   (3)
Statue of Liberty   18
stay   (15)
stay at   18
stay home   15
steak   (7)
still (adv)   (14)
stomach   12
stomachache   12
stop (v)   (7)
stop (n)   (17)
store   6
street (st.)   3
student   1
study   4
study for   (4)
stuffy   12
subway   (18)
sugar   7
suggest   (4)
suit   16
summer   (7), 13
Sunday   3
super discount   (7)
supermarket   6
sure   (5), 7
swim   5
swiss cheese   (10)

T

T-shirt   16
tablespoon   9
tablet   (12)
take   16
take care   1
take care of   8
take out   1
talented   (5)
talk   (6)

tall 17
taste 9
taxi 17
tea 7
teach 8
teacher (3), 8
team (8)
teaspoon (9)
technical institute (7), 8
telephone company 3
telephone number 3
telephone operator 2
temperature (13)
ten 1
tennis (4)
tenth 5
terrible 12
terrific 8
test (7)
thanks 1
thank you 1
that 2
that's 2
that's fine 7
the 2
theater 6
their 2
then 12
there 3
these 2
they 2
they're 2
thing (5)
third 5
thirsty 10
thirteen 1
thirteenth 5
thirtieth 5
thirty 2
thirty-first 5
this 1
this week 15
three 1
throat 12
through 8
Thursday 3
ticket 12
tie 16
time 4
tired (10), 12

to 1
toasted (10)
today 1
told (12)
tomato 7
tomato paste (9)
tomorrow 1
tonight 1
too (5), 16
too bad 4
took 18
tooth 12
toothache 12
top (18)
town (10)
trade (18)
train 17
train station 6
travel (7), 11
travel agent 1
trip 17
Tuesday 3
tuna (10)
turkey (7)
turn on (8)
TV 4
TV guide (8)
twelfth 5
twelve 1
twentieth 5
twenty 1
twenty-eight 2
twenty-eighth 5
twenty-fifth 5
twenty-first 5
twenty-five 2
twenty-four 2
twenty-fourth 5
twenty-nine 2
twenty-ninth 5
twenty-one 2
twenty-second 5
twenty-seven 2
twenty-seventh 5
twenty-six 2
twenty-sixth 5
twenty-third 5
twenty-three 2
twenty-two 2
two 1

typical (10), 11

## U

uh 5
understand 6
United States 5
university (6)
us 4
use 9
usually (6), 13

## V

vacation 17
vanilla (9)
varies (13)
vegetable 7
very 5
Vietnam 5
Vietnamese 5
view (18)
village (18)
violin 5
visa (17)
visit (5)
voice (3)
volleyball 5

## W

wait a minute (8)
waiter 10
waitress 10
walk 17
want + (n) (6), 10
warm 13
warning (12)
was/were 13
wash 4
watch (v) 4
watch (n) 4
water 10
watermelon (7)
way 16
we 2
wear 16
weather 13
Wednesday 3

## PHOTO CREDITS

page 53 *(left)* Wide World Photos, Inc.
page 53 *(right)* UPI/Bettmann Newsphotos
page 54 *(top left)* © Bob Daemmrich/The Image Works
page 54 *(A)* Sam Sweezy/Stock, Boston
page 54 *(B)* © Bob Daemmrich/Stock, Boston
page 54 *(C)* Cary Wolinsky/Stock, Boston
page 54 *(bottom)* Wide World Photos, Inc.
page 120 Gary T. Byrne
page 173 © Jan Halaska/The Image Works

A special thanks to Corena Harwell of Lancaster, Texas,
for the use of her photo on page 54.